Stop Parenting & Start Coaching

Stop Parenting & Start Coaching will take your relationship with your teenager to a higher level. These authors not only understand teens, they have given teens a voice. This book teaches parents how to be more effective by listening with their hearts, not just their ears.

—*James Malinchak, Contributing Editor,* Chicken Soup for the Teenage Soul *and author of* Teenagers Tips for Success

Finally, a book on parenting teens that makes sense and can actually help even the best parent to navigate the teenage years! Most parents are pleased if they can just "maintain" a relationship with their teen. This book, if put into practice, can prevent parenting disasters, restore damaged relationships, and build bridges for lifelong communication with your children. This might be the parenting manual that we've all been waiting for. It is a must read for every parent!

—*Dr. Richard Simpson, Assistant Superintendent of Instruction, Conejo Valley Unified School District*

The authors have put together a clear, compelling, and easy-to-read book that will move you to shift from that old "father/mother knows best" style of parenting to one that is far more effective—one that calls forth the resourcefulness and creativeness of your teens, calling them to display the innate greatness they all contain.

—*Ann Kerr Romberg, CPCC, Life & Business Coach*

Principled behavior is the key to parenting, teaching, coaching, and managing. Despite being trained in these principles, those in charge often make emotional decisions that bring unintended effects. *Stop Parenting* gives, in memorable story form, a realistic look at reactive as well as principled responses to adolescents, thereby giving the parent, and by analogy the teacher, an indelible model. Parents and teachers will benefit, but not as much as the children.

—Dr. Frank Lyman, Ph.D., Professor Emeritus,
University of Maryland and Howard County Public Schools

I wish I had had this book when my kids were adolescents. It lands squarely on most of the major issues you face as the parent of teens in a story format that's easy to follow.

—Wayne Kuna, parent, Kuna & Associates, Toy Company

LifeBound's new book, *Stop Parenting & Stop Coaching,* offers a fresh perspective on how to be more effective and influential in your teen's life. As a family counselor, I will recommend my clients read this. The practical advice in this book can be applied to just about any parenting situation.

—Tim Nordberg, Executive Director, Hope for the Family

From the first time I picked it up, I was surprised by how interesting and relevant this book was to me. As a college freshman, I didn't expect to be so captivated by a book on parenting. It's great to know that someone finally understands the real issues at work between teenagers and their parents.

—Kelly Carson, student, University of Kansas

Stop Parenting & Start Coaching

How to Motivate, Inspire, and Connect with Your Teenager

Carol Carter
Gary Izumo
Joe Martin

Michael Robertson
DEVELOPMENTAL EDITOR

LifeBound

DENVER, COLORADO

Dedication

This book is dedicated to parents and teenagers everywhere who seek to understand each other, bring out the best in themselves, and commit to becoming the people that they want to be in the world.

LifeBound
1600 Broadway
Suite 2400
Denver, Colorado 80202

ISBN 0–9742044–0–4

10 9 8 7 6 5 4 3 2 1

Printed in the United States of America.

CONTENTS

ACKNOWLEDGMENTS

We are grateful to the insights of many people who spent countless hours helping us to develop this manuscript. We are blessed to have the opportunity to work with so many people whose passion and commitment to parents and teens are unwavering.

Michael Robertson, our developmental editor, was instrumental in developing the creative writing that shaped our chapters. His diligence and flexibility allowed us to work well within our time frame and maintain the focus to keep moving forward.

We spoke with scores of teens, parents, teachers and coaches who provided their wisdom. We wish to thank all of them, including the following individuals:

Mary Jane Bradbury

Deirdre Dalton-Brodeur

Robyn Collins

Cynthia Dormer, Ph.D., R.D.

George Fifield

Ann Goss

David Goss

Elizabeth Izumo

Susan Izumo

Wayne Kuna

A.J. Lopez

Frank Lyman, Ph.D.

Eileen Mahoney

Lynn Montrose

Shana Montrose

Cynthia Nordberg

Tim Nordberg

Ann Romberg

Eric Schmitt

Gail Simpson

Richard Simpson

Richard Thompson

Suzanne Thompson

Karen Timmons, Ph.D.

Frank Timmons, Ph.D.

Rita Trumbo

Finally, we want to thank our families for their patience, love, support, and commitment throughout this process and always. We are inspired by your faith in us.

Congratulations!

The following pages provide a summary of and quick reference to the most important points of our book.

Remember . . .

While the issues haven't changed, our teenagers have.

We have to work with teens, not against them.

Teenagers respond to respect by showing respect. Teens are quick to listen to anyone who listens to them.

Every teen is different, and some strategies will work better than others. Keep doing what works, and stop doing what doesn't.

It's impossible to work on a problem or challenge without first admitting that you have one.

You can weather any problem with your teen as long as you're clear that there is a foundation of love for the relationship.

About Parenting

You don't have to apologize for being a responsible parent.

Teens are more likely to do as you do than as you say. Parents need to practice what they preach and lead by example.

The toughest thing about being a parent is learning when not *to be one.*

About Feelings

The very nature of being a parent can be enough to make a teen feel great anger toward you.

It's not your job to retaliate against your teen's anger.

Your teen is your child, but she is also her own person. Allow her to express her feelings, while at the same time admitting your own.

Your child's feelings are just as valid as your own. You can't argue with your child's feelings, you can only question them (their feelings) and try to better understand them.

Parents are programmed to react in certain ways to certain behaviors, in much the way teens are programmed to rebel against authority.

About Communication

Regardless of what happens between you and your teenager, always keep the lines of communication open.

The problem in dealing with teenagers is one of strategy: the strategy parents use to communicate.

The main set of skills that parents have to develop is listening skills.

About Change

Admit that you might need some help. You need to be a willing participant in change in order to effect it.

In order to change anything, you must first change your own attitude about it.

You can't expect to change others without first changing yourself.

About Motivation

The only effective motivation to change is self-motivation.

By asking why, you can discover what truly motivates your teen.

The important thing about helping your teen find his passion is that it opens so many doors to personal development, maturity, and fulfillment.

To help a teen find her own way, be encouraging and supportive, and provide resources.

About Success

No one can make you feel like a failure as a parent without your consent.

Realize that the appearance of parenting success is not the same as being a successful parent.

Since you get what you focus on in life, rather than focusing on failing as a parent, try to focus on succeeding as one.

The Difference Between a Parent and a Coach

Parents usually tell *teens what to do, while coaches try to* show *them.*

Parents try to protect *their teens, while coaches try to* prepare *them.*

Parents often decide *what's best for their teens, while coaches would rather* let them learn *from the consequences of their own decisions.*

Parents want their teens to like *them, while coaches want to* be respected.

Parents offer love *to teens, while coaches offer* tough love.

Parents often remind *teens of their failures, while coaches* build on *those failures.*

Parents are often afraid *to trust teens, while coaches have* no choice *but to trust them.*

Questions to Ask Yourself About Your Teen

What kind of problem is your teen having with you?

What does your teen think about the situation, and why would she think that?

What might your teenager say about you to his best friends, when you're not around?

The Three Most Common Fears of Parents

1. *The fear of their teen having to struggle, or to make "life" mistakes.*

2. *The fear that their teen will become dependent on them, or others, in order to survive.*

3. *The fear that their children will not succeed in life, and that they—the parents—will be blamed for it.*

Steps to Moving Through Fears

The first step is to identify the fear.

The next step is to move into and evaluate the fear.

The third step is to move through the fear.

Steps to Overcoming Parenting Fears

1. Write down three adjectives you would like your teen-ager to use in describing you as a parent.

2. Under each of those adjectives, list the reasons why it is important to you.

3. Evaluate where you are now as a parent: Are you moving closer to or farther away from the adjectives you listed in Step 1?

4. Make a list of the things you can do to move even closer to the kind of parent you described in Step 1.

5. Make a commitment to do one thing a week from the list you made in Step 4.

Questions for Evaluating a Past Situation

1. What did you do right?

2. What did you do wrong?

3. What did you really fear? Why did you really react the way you did?

4. What opportunities did you miss to build a bridge with your teen?

5. What did you learn?

6. What's the best possible thing you could have done to handle the situation better? Now do it!

Questions to Help Teens Reach Their Own Self-Directed Goals

What is your passion?

What is it about these activities that gets you excited?

What kind of activities and professions relate to your passion?

Who are some individuals who are professionally involved in your passion?

What do you think these people were like as children, as teens, or as college students?

How do you think the parents and teachers of these people would have described them?

Would you like to find out more about these people, so you can understand how they got to where they are?

Would you like to do some research on this together?

The Biggest Grievances Teens Have About Their Parents

1. *That parents try to make decisions for them.*

2. *That parents are too controlling.*

3. *That parents are overprotective.*

4. *That parents try to live vicariously through them.*

5. *That a parent's love sometimes feels conditional.*

6. *That parents have unrealistic expectations, or that they expect perfection.*

7. *That parents project their own fears and insecurities on their children.*

8. *That parents don't practice what they preach.*

OWN THE PROBLEM

Gaining Focus

September 2

"I hate you!"

The words reverberated through Greg's whole being. His daughter had just screamed at him something he'd hoped he'd never hear. He felt stung, angry, and sad. He tried *not* to feel defeated. Of course he'd heard of teen angst before, and Greg felt no reason to believe he or his daughter should be immune to any of life's challenges, but he just didn't think it would be this hard. He could still see Kelly in the delivery room the first time he held her. He saw her leaning over the Big Bird birthday cake her mother had baked for her third birthday. He remembered the way her eyes lit up like the candles, her smile gleaming as she blew them out, the warm feeling shared between all three of them.

Lately, though, all they had done was fight. And Greg couldn't let this latest remark slide.

"You don't hate *me,*" he said to Kelly, "you hate yourself. Look at the way you sulk around and blame everyone else for *your* problems. You're acting like a four-year-old!"

"Oh, right. And you're acting like an adult?" Kelly shouted. Her eyes were narrow, nose crumpled up. She shot a look of scorn at her father, as though she thought she could see right through him.

Greg felt his temples flush. "Don't you talk to me that way, young lady! I'm your father."

"Some father," she said, sneering. "Always telling me what to do. School this! Job that! It's like you think you own me."

An overwhelming rage rushed over Greg, tightening his muscles and causing his breath to come in quick, short bursts. Who was *she* to talk this way to *him?* Hadn't *he* worked two jobs to put himself through college? Didn't he and his wife put in 40 and 50 hours a week to pay bills *and* buy clothes *and* put food on the table? He'd given his whole life to his children, and now Kelly was trying to walk all over him, as if his sacrifices meant nothing.

"That's enough!" he shouted.

"No–it–is–not–enough!" Kelly shot back, enunciating each word as if she were speaking to a child. "You never listen to me. You think you know just the way everything's supposed to be. You don't care what anyone else thinks!"

"My house, my rules!" Greg roared. The kitchen suddenly felt much too small for the two of them. He knew he was on the verge of saying something he'd regret, and yet he was allowing his anger to get the best of him. "Someday when you're the parent," he said, "then you can make the rules."

Tears welled up in Kelly's eyes. "I hate it here!" she yelled. "I hate *you!*" Her cheeks were flushed.

Greg raised a single finger in warning, and through clenched teeth spit the words: "You are grounded, you little ingrate!"

"I don't care!" Kelly retorted.

As soon as the first tear began to roll down Kelly's cheek, Greg felt instantly embarrassed. He knew he wanted to be a better father than this; he just wasn't sure how.

The door slammed shut on this thought—a loud crack awakening Greg to the fact that his daughter had just run from the house.

*   *   *

That slam made Greg feel like a man who had painted himself into a corner. The smile that loomed above the Big Bird birthday cake seemed to have all but disappeared. His daughter had been a strange creature lately—part playful child, doodling sunsets in her journal while lying on the lawn, and part hard-boiled cynic. It was like an alien had come and invaded his daughter's mind.

She was the same beautiful, intelligent child he helped raise from birth. But her smarts seemed to have faded from their natural inquisitive playfulness, leaning toward the crafty and cunning, and her radiant smiles had given way to curled lips, piercing stares, and unabashed apathy. She saw his naked attempts at reconciliation as weakness, and imposition of strong-willed parenting as tyranny. Greg felt lost no matter what he did, defeated no matter what his intentions.

If he tried a gentle reminder that she should study, Kelly would often yell that it was her own business, then lock herself in the bathroom for an hour and do her hair. Other days she'd leave the house with her hair wet—despite a cough or scratchy throat. She seemed to care more about her appearance than her grades, more about her social life than her health, and no matter what Greg said to his daughter she almost always replied that he "didn't understand." She acted as if becoming a teenager meant an automatic drop of 50 points in his IQ as a parent. Greg had never felt frustration quite like this before.

When his wife Kathy walked into the kitchen, arriving home from a long day at the office, Greg realized he couldn't go on like this.

"Hi sweetie, what's up?" she asked.

"Another knock-down, drag-out fight with Kelly. I guess she'll just go off to college in two years and then hate me for the rest of her life." Greg was starting to identify with the cynic his daughter had become, a thought that caused him more than a little concern.

"Sounds like you're going down the road of the victim. Is that what you really want to do?"

"Sorry, you're right," Greg said.

When Kathy asked if Kelly was in her room, Greg just nodded, preferring not to mention the guilt he felt over chasing his own daughter out of the house. But then again he'd simply *tried* to get through to her, and if he didn't know *exactly* how, then that could scarcely be considered a crime.

"Is her door locked again?" Kathy asked.

Again Greg nodded.

"Honey," she said, "I've got a suggestion that I want you to consider, even though you haven't been open to help in the past. This is becoming a pattern. You're both growing more and more frustrated." Kathy scrutinized his face, looking for any sign of misgiving. Greg's eyes were wide, pleading for any suggestion that might work. "I ran into Megan Trujillo at lunch. Apparently she and Brian have a wonderful friend who's really helped them get through to their son. He's acted as a coach, a parenting coach for them."

"A 'parenting coach'?" Greg asked.

"Yeah, you know, someone who helps provide guidance. Their friend helped them be more effective parents for their son. He was able to provide an outside perspective based on his experience working with kids and resolving family conflict." Greg sighed, and Kathy continued. "Apparently Megan and Brian were going crazy with their youngest. The school was calling every day, his grades were poor, and they were having problems with him at home. Megan said their friend has some really amazing strategies. She said it really worked and was worth the investment."

"I don't know," Greg said. He felt hesitant, somehow preferring to believe that a father must surely know best.

"I do know," Kathy said. "Remember when I took those personal improvement seminars last year? Those strategies I learned got me out of the slump I'd been in. I felt better, more confident. I finally got that promotion I'd wanted for so long. I've always believed that if you're not willing to do the personal work, nothing ever changes." She paused and placed her hand over her husband's. "Greg, honey. I really need you to do this for me, for Kelly, for all of us. I'm carrying my own stresses and we can't keep going around the same tracks. What's the worst that can happen if you try this?"

"I'm not sure," Greg said. "Talk to a stranger?"

"Hey, my seminar leader was a stranger. What have you got to lose? *Really*. We both need some help with Kelly. Try it once with an open mind. If you like what this 'coach' has to say, and think it might help, then maybe you could teach me and we'd all be better off. If you don't, we can try something else. It's in your court, but we need to find a strategy that works and commit to it."

Greg looked away for a moment. He hated the emotional roller coaster it sometimes seemed their lives had become. He hated feeling like he had to walk on eggshells around his own daughter, and he knew he was creating more stress for the whole family. As he felt Kathy squeeze his hand, it was this thought that prompted him to speak.

"You know what?" he said, just barely allowing himself to smile.

"What?"

"I knew there was a good reason that I married you."
Kathy smiled back. "Then you'll try it?" she asked.
Greg nodded.

"I knew there was a good reason I married you, too."

What to Remember

- *Different and sometimes difficult behaviors in teens are normal and require different skills from those needed in the pre-teen years.*

- *Have the courage to reach out to others—don't try to be an island of responsibility. Sharing concerns and seeking "outside" perspectives allow you to gain strength and new insights.*

2

THINK LIKE A COACH

Shifting Perspective

September 20

In her journal, Kelly wrote:

I'm so sick of arguing with my parents! It's like I can't say anything without it being a major issue. Every little thing I say or do is always wrong. Always! When I do something really well, like get an A on a test or something, Dad always acts like that was just what he expected. But if I bring home a C or something, then it's World War III. Even Mom gets on my back. Always yelling at me to pick up my clothes—in my own room! And I hate the way she nags about unplugging the hair dryer. As if I'm going to throw it in the sink while I'm brushing my teeth! They just have way too many rules! Why can't they realize that I'm doing the best I can and be proud that I'm trying? I don't know. I do feel bad that I told Dad I hate him a few weeks ago. I mean, I guess I meant it in the moment, but I know I shouldn't have said it. And I know I don't really mean it. But how can I take something like that back when bringing it up will probably just get me lectured? I can just see it now, "Dad, you know when I said that I hated you?" Then he'd blow up again, and I wouldn't even get the chance to apologize. And all this just makes Billy look like the perfect child. He makes mistakes too. But he's younger, and doesn't have all the pressure of high school. What could he screw up? Forget to put his bike away. Forget to put in his retainer. Big deal. They don't yell about those things, but that's like the hardest thing they expect from him. I wish it was that easy! High school's hard, and (I hate to admit it) there's pressure to be cool. I can't wait until I'm out on my own and making all my own decisions. Maybe things will finally get a little easier. I'm going shopping to escape this hellhole.

*   *   *

As Greg drove toward the coffee shop where he and Vince had agreed to meet, he found himself feeling torn inside. On the one hand he would do anything to help his family. *Of course he would.* But on the other, he wasn't used to spilling his guts—especially to a stranger. However, his wife made a big point of how important it was to be brutally honest with this guy in order to get something out of it.

Greg and Kelly hadn't spoken since their last big fight, and Kathy's attempts at levity had fallen flat. To his wife's joking that their house had turned into an "Ice Palace," Kelly and Greg just grimaced. They stared straight ahead at their plates, and continued to eat in silence. The conflict hounded Greg, and it was for that very reason he'd felt it was the right move to get the number of the Trujillos' friend and set a meeting.

Vince had been very cordial on the phone, explaining that since he had retired, parent coaching had become something of a hobby for him. It gave him the gratification he no longer received from a hard day's work. And since Greg and Kathy were such good friends of the Trujillo family, Vince agreed to see what he could do to help.

Greg pulled into a parking spot and walked into the coffee shop. After ordering a cup of coffee he looked around until he saw a man in a red cap, which Vince said he'd be wearing. Approaching the man, Greg asked, "Vince?"

"And you must be Greg," Vince said, extending a hand. "Care to take a seat?"

The two men shook hands and Greg sat down at the table.

"Teens can be a real pain, can't they?" Vince said.

Greg laughed.

"Listen," Vince went on, "I think I understand a little about why you're here, so let me start with a little about myself. I'm also a father—three kids, all grown. I worked as a manager of human resources for sixteen years, and then became a career counselor. I retired five years ago.

"When my oldest son was in the second grade, I started coaching his Little League team." Vince had a twinkle in his eye, as if he could still see his son trying to swing his way to the championship. "What I noticed in motivating those little boys to do the calisthenics, to run the laps and practice the drills—to be the best they could be, really—was that I couldn't make them do it. Yelling only produced sloppy results. They had to want it—for *themselves*. I racked my brain to think of some way to get these kids moving, and found myself calling on some of my business strategies for managing employees, as well as career strategies aimed at helping people reach their goals. They really worked! In the end, Greg, I learned that managing employees, coaching the team, and parenting are virtually one and the same. At least as far as how we approach problems and find resolutions.

"But we can get into all this in much more detail later. Let me first ask you a question, Greg. What brings you here today?"

"Well, like I told you on the phone, my wife and I have been having problems with our daughter, Kelly."

"I realize that," Vince told him. "What I want to know is what brings *you* here?"

"Well, I guess I'm here because my daughter hates me." As Greg said this he could feel a tightness in the pit of his stomach.

"I'm sure that's not the case," Vince said, smiling. "But I'm also sure that you often feel that way. Tell me more about why that might be."

"Ever been referred to as Attila the Hun? How about 'the worst parent on the face of the planet'? I've loved and raised and lived with this child, and just last week she told me she hated me. I don't mind a challenge, but sometimes this feels like a nightmare. The thing is, I'm really starting to feel like I'm losing her. I really do want a strong relationship with my daughter, not just now, but for the rest of our lives. And when she blows off her chores or tells me she hates me, that sometimes feels impossible. Sometimes I have to jog around the block just to get the rage out of my system. Plus, I have my own frustrations at work these days, which give me an even shorter fuse at home. My department has been downsized and I'm now doing the work of three people without an assistant. Fortunately, I've missed two rounds of layoffs, but it has been a pressure cooker." Greg threw his hands in the air in frustration.

Vince listened compassionately, nodding in understanding. "Of course, Greg. I definitely understand. As a parenting coach—working with parents and teens—I've seen my share of anger and troubles. And believe it or not, I've also had my own share of sleepless nights because of it."

"You have? But don't you deal with hard-to-manage, unmotivated teens all the time?"

Vince nodded, not bothering to hide his smile. "Of course I do. But believe it or not, the teens aren't the ones giving me insomnia. Most of the time it's their parents."

Now Greg smiled, leaning forward. "Okay, okay," he said, "I get it. Reverse psychology. So what is it you're trying to say?"

"Just that." Vince shrugged. "That it's usually the parents who are keeping me up at night. Or in other words, the most cause for concern."

"Really," Greg said, trying not to raise his voice. He hadn't, after all, come here to be insulted, but he knew that he was overly sensitive to criticism.

"Why don't you let me ask you a few questions?"

Greg nodded. "Fine."

"First off: What kind of problem is your teen having with you?"

Greg paused, taken aback. "Problems she's having with me?"

"Yeah."

"Besides the fact that she thinks I'm a dictator?" he said. "I guess that I don't want her to have any fun."

"Why would she think that?"

Greg coughed, then continued. "Because she says that I treat her like a little girl."

"Think of an example."

"She says I try to tell her what to wear, who her friends should be, that I'm overprotective and unfair, that I have too many rules."

"Is there anything else that could contribute to her feelings?"

"She says that I never listen to her, that I always think I'm right, that she's always wrong. She says I think she's too young to understand, that I don't value her opinion. I hate for her to feel that way, but I'm just trying to help her be well-rounded and motivated."

"You don't have to apologize for being a responsible parent."

"It's just that sometimes I really do think she hates me," Greg said, taking a deep breath. "I try to understand sometimes what she really thinks. Sometimes I wonder if she might occasionally be justified. My temper *can* be difficult to put up with, and sometimes I feel like raising a child is a guessing game anyway. How am I supposed to know if I am making all the right choices?"

"Is that all, Greg? What else concerns you?"

"I suppose—or at least all I can think of at the moment."

"Well," Vince said, rubbing his hands together. "That's a start. Now, I want you to imagine that I'm one of your daughter's best friends. In order to understand what your teen thinks about you, ask yourself what she might say to her best friends, when you're not around."

"That's a good question," Greg said. "I guess I never really thought about that." He leaned forward, looking right at Vince. "I guess she might say something like: 'He's trying to control my life, what I spend, how and when I use my cell phone, what I wear, how I look, who I see, how I talk, what I listen to, where I go, what I do, when I do it, how I do it, I mean everything.' She'd probably tell them that I make her angry, make her want to go crazy."

"What else might she say?"

"She might say that she can't wait until she's old enough to move out on her own, 'so that I'll never have to listen to him or do what he says anymore. When I have children I'll never treat them the way he treats me.'" With this Greg finally went silent, his eyes trailing off toward the ground.

"Congratulations!" Vince said, beaming.

"Congratulations?" Greg asked. "For what? For raising a teenager who hates my guts?"

"Congratulations for having a normal teenager."

Greg shook his head. "Okay, I've had enough with the reverse psychology," he said. "What are you really trying to say?"

"The very nature of being a parent can be enough to make a teen feel great anger toward you. It doesn't make your child's feelings right or wrong, but you have to recognize that those feelings are *real*. She may be your daughter, but she is also her own person. Allow her to express herself, her feelings, while at the same time admitting to your own, and you may find that an open dialogue is easier to establish than you thought. Communication is the key to a healthy relationship with your child."

"So," Greg said, scratching his head. "No joke? You're telling me that my daughter's feelings are normal?"

"Absolutely! I've talked to dozens of parents, and most of them admit that their own teens would probably say similar things about them. This is just the nature of a parent/child relationship. Your child's feelings are just as valid as your own. You can't argue with these emotions. You can only question and try to understand them."

"Question them?" Greg said with an underlying intensity in his voice. "That's just the excuse she looks for to blow up."

"Now hold on a minute," Vince said, raising a finger in the air. "Let me give you a 'for instance.' I could have called you and your wife, suggesting that you need outside help with your child. However, did I call you?"

"No. I called you."

"Exactly! You called me because you're *questioning* your child's feelings. Arguing over them with her was no longer proving effective. You've taken an important first step here, which is to admit that you need some help. You need to be a willing participant in order to effect a change. The role of forced bystander gets you nowhere. I won't be able to give you answers to your problems, but I can ask some questions that will help you uncover the answers on your own. This is what we call 'coaching,' or question-asking, and it's the basis for everything I'll share with you in coaching and communicating with your teen."

"I'm still not sure exactly what you mean by 'coaching' my teenager. Do you mean like athletics?"

"Somewhat," Vince said, "but not exactly. I'll explain coaching in more detail in just a minute. But for now, let me ask you another question: Remember when I told you that my greatest challenge as a coach isn't usually the teenager, but rather the parent?"

"Yes, and I still don't understand why."

"What I've found from coaching teens is that teenagers are quicker to admit and acknowledge their mistakes than adults are. They're also quicker to work on correcting those mistakes. Teens are more open and honest with their emotions: They're quicker to forgive, quicker to admit when they don't know something, quicker to try new things, and most important, they're quicker to seek outside help, whether it's from their peers or anyone else who will listen. My apologies for sounding trite, Greg, but kids are like sponges: They love to take things in. I honestly only wish more adults were like that." He paused, then went on:

"Teens today have major issues and challenges—we *all* do—but it's important to remember that teenagers respond to respect by showing respect. They're more likely to do as you do, rather than as you say. Parents need to practice what they preach and lead by example in order to get their children to listen. Teens are quick to listen to anyone who listens to them. That's not always sound logic on their part, but it is part of the process of maturing. Adults listen, too. However, what slows us down in our development is that we're reluctant to admit that we even have a problem, let alone seek help for one. In spite of the challenges you face with your teen, you've already made the necessary first step. It takes a lot of courage to admit things aren't right—especially in your own home—and then seek help from an outsider. Most people would rather sweep their problems under the rug, and then blame everyone else for them. Eventually, though, if the problems continue to pile up, the lump under the rug becomes more and more obvious to anyone who knows you. And nevertheless, some people still choose to ignore the problem."

"What you're saying is that it's impossible to work on a problem, or 'challenge,' without first admitting that you have one."

"Absolutely. Now here's another question: Have you noticed that I haven't asked you what *you* thought was wrong with your daughter?"

"I suppose, but I just assumed you'd ask me eventually."

"Well, I won't. Do you know why?"

"If I had to take a guess, I'd say it's because my opinion would be biased."

"You're close, but not exactly," Vince said. "See, it really doesn't matter what *you* think your daughter's problems are. The only thing that matters is what *she* thinks her problems are. This doesn't mean that, as a parent, you won't know what her shortcomings are, that you're wrong about her struggles, or that I don't value your opinion. The truth of the matter is that I'm not going to help you 'fix' your daughter. What I hope to do is help you work on *you,* so that you can effectively help your daughter to make the most of her gifts, talents, and abilities, despite the inevitable impasses in your relationship."

"I'm not totally clear on all this."

Vince leaned back in his seat. "Let me provide some perspective on the coaching process," he said. "The most common complaint I hear from parents when it comes to dealing with their teenager is: 'I don't know what's wrong with my teen.' You've come to me with a similar attitude.

And just like I asked you, I ask all parents I work with to explain what brought them to me. Parents tend to respond by saying things like: 'I can't get him to do anything without making threats. He does whatever he wants, whenever he wants, like he's intentionally disobeying me. I wish there was something I could do to motivate him, to help him be more responsible, make better decisions, and listen better.'"

Greg gave a nervous laugh. "It sounds like you've been eavesdropping at my house."

"Didn't I tell you that your daughter is perfectly normal? These are common concerns for most parents.

"I'd like to reiterate that the problem usually isn't the teenager. Teen issues are basically the same today as they always were. The problem in dealing with teenagers is one of strategy, namely, the strategy parents use to communicate with their teens. I'm sure you've heard the saying: 'If you keep doing what you've always done, you'll keep getting what you've always gotten.'"

"Yeah," Greg told him. "My wife says that to me all the time."

"Well, it's true. A lot of parents are using the same strategies they've always used with their teens, and yet they're expecting different results. Times have changed, and so have teenagers. Even if teen issues haven't changed much—anything from sex to drugs, friends, grades, and peer pressure—teenagers themselves have changed dramatically. Today's teenagers are more savvy and sophisticated than we ever were at their age. Many teens today know more, but think less; most are more experienced, but less mature; they may do more, but behave less responsibly. Sometimes it honestly doesn't seem to make any sense.

"In our day, promising rewards and threatening punishment may have been reliable methods of motivation, but these methods have become outdated and ineffective, just as the hierarchical structure in business has been replaced with the 'flattened' organization, where management is driven more by consensus building and participation and less by directive.

"In short, while the issues haven't changed, our teenagers have. Unfortunately, the thinking and strategizing of many parents, teachers, and others who work with teens haven't adjusted to the change. We're just human. It is easier to stay comfortable in the familiar rather than change. But when our own way of thinking becomes calcified, and we refuse to recognize the need for change, matters only get worse.

"And so, in terms of parenting, I've proposed an old, but new strategy."

"What do you mean by 'old, but new'?" Greg asked.

"Old in the sense of the strategy itself, but new in the sense of the context in which it's applied."

Greg leaned forward. "Are you referring to 'question-asking'?"

"I am. People sometimes refer to this skill as parent coaching, but it involves many abilities, from question-asking to championing to listening.

"You see, the toughest thing about being a parent is learning when *not* to be one. It can be hard to know when to let go and when to stand firm. Of course, you need to respect your child's uniqueness, but you also must strive to protect her from developing habits that might hurt her in life. With MTV, the Internet, movies, and music, today's teenagers see, hear, and do more than we ever dreamed of doing—and at an even earlier age. New teenagers require new strategies. I believe today's teens need more question-asking, brainstorming, and strategy, and less 'parenting' in the traditional sense of the word.

"Have you ever participated in organized sports?"

"Yeah," Greg said, "I sure did. In high school I was a wrestler."

"And did you have a good coach?"

"One of the best in our state," Greg told him. "He always had our team ranked among the top five in the state, and I'll tell you that he certainly got the best out of me."

"Got the best out of you?" Vince asked. "What do you mean?"

"You should've seen me my freshman year in high school," Greg mused. "I was scrawny, didn't have much self-confidence, and my wrestling skills were a joke. Somehow, my coach helped me become one of the best in my weight class. I *still* can't believe it!"

"This is the type of transformational change I'm talking about. That experience is going to make what I'm about to share with you a whole lot easier to grasp."

"Okay, I'm all ears," Greg said.

Vince waited a moment and then responded, "All right, let's start with this. What attributes come to mind when you think of your coach?"

"Well . . . first of all, he always believed in me, even when I doubted myself. When I told him what I wanted to accomplish, he challenged me to set my goals higher. And through everything, he always trusted me."

"Trusted you?"

"He'd make me responsible for certain things that were really important to the team."

"What else?"

"He always led by example. He'd get on the mat with us to show us new moves. He'd do laps with us in the scorching heat. I even remember once when I complained about a boring class I was struggling in, he actually came to my class, sat in for the entire period, and took notes. Then he gave me some suggestions on how I could do better in class, like sit in the front, ask questions, build rapport with the teacher, and so forth."

"Why do you think he did that, Greg?"

"To show me that a boring class is no excuse for poor grades."

"And how did you do in the class?"

"I got a B once I became more active."

"Anything else?"

"He was tough on me when I screwed up, but he always pulled me aside to tell me why."

"What reasons did he give for his toughness?" Vince asked.

"He'd pull out the goals I'd set for myself at the beginning of the semester and remind me that it was his job to make sure I achieved every one of them, even if it made me mad at him."

"What else do you remember about him?"

"Well, he'd always ask us what we thought about something. Whether it was a particular opponent, discipline for another wrestler, or even the color scheme for the new uniforms, he always asked for our feedback. Even if he didn't use our ideas, he always asked for them. I respected him for that."

"Anything else?"

"I'm sure there is, but that's what I remember best about him."

"As you listen to what I'm about to say, think about how you relate your relationship with your coach to your role as a parent. Be totally honest with yourself."

"All right."

"Typically, when it comes to parenting and coaching, my observation has been:

- "Parents usually *tell* teens what to do, while coaches try to *show* them;

- "Parents try to *protect* their teens, while coaches try to *prepare* them;

- "Parents often *decide* what's best for their teens, while coaches would rather *let them learn* from the consequences of their own decisions;

- "Parents want their teens to *like* them, while coaches want to be *respected*;

- "Parents offer *love* to teens, while coaches offer *tough love;*

- "Parents often *remind* teens of their failures, while coaches *build on* those failures;

- "Parents are often *afraid to trust* teens, while coaches have *no choice* but to trust them.

"Can you relate to any of these things, Greg?"

"Unfortunately, yes. I never looked at it that way before, but now I can see why I respected my coach so much. He helped me to get the most out of my natural abilities. So, is that what's wrong with me? That I'm smothering my daughter?"

"No, Greg. The problem isn't you. The problem is the strategy you're using with your daughter.

"It's the same strategy that most parents have been using for years. Parenthood doesn't come with an instruction book. You've just done the best you could with the resources you've had. Believe me, there are a lot of parents out there who are using the wrong strategies when it comes to motivating and connecting with teenagers.

"Remember: In order to change anything, you must first change your own attitude about it. You'll accomplish nothing by pitting yourself against Kelly. The only way for things to improve is for you to work *with* her. And that's why I'm here—to help you gain a new perspective on your problem, or should I say, your 'challenge' of better connecting with your daughter.

"When I ask parents what they want most for their child, the response is almost unanimously: 'I want my child to be happy.' Unfortunately, 'happy' usually translates into: 'I want my child to do what I want him to do, when I want him to do it, how I want him to do it, and then *I* will be happy.'

"When teenagers don't respond the way we expect them to, we often claim they're being rebellious, unmotivated, or irresponsible, or that they're refusing to listen. The truth is that instead of giving our teens what *they need*, we're trying to force them to do what *we want*. That, in itself, isn't necessarily a bad thing, since most teens would rather do what feels good as opposed to what is actually good for them. But as I've said: We have to work with our teens, not against them.

"Again, that's where parent coaching comes in. There is a way to give your teen what she needs, and at the same time help her to get what she wants. It sounds difficult, but it's not. It's actually fairly simple, although it's not easy. But it requires a new set of skills that most parents haven't fully developed, the main one being listening skills."

"You mean that I'll get my daughter on track just by listening?" Greg asked.

"Not exactly," Vince responded. "I think one of the biggest misconceptions when it comes to human development is that we can 'motivate' other people. I tend to disagree with that. I don't really believe you can motivate anyone else. We, as humans, do things for our own reasons, and not for anyone else's. Of course you can threaten and coerce someone into doing almost anything, but that's not motivation. That's persuasion, manipulation, or worse, intimidation. But if a person is truly motivated, she won't need outside prodding; she'll achieve on her own, and continue to do so, even when you're not telling her or making her do it. What I'm saying is really quite simple: There is only one type of effective motivation for us to change, and that's self-motivation.

"For instance, let's say your daughter doesn't study when she's supposed to, and you're constantly reminding her to do it. What do you think most parents would do to convince their teenager to study?"

Greg scratched his head and thought for a moment before responding. "I think most parents would threaten to take away something that's important to the child. Maybe they would create negative consequences if their teen doesn't study."

"Do you think this strategy will work?"

"Well, it depends."

"Depends on what?"

"It depends on the teenager and the parent. If the teenager is anything like my daughter, it probably won't make much difference what you try to tell her to do, or take from her. On the other hand, if the teen really values this privilege, she'll probably heed the warning and study. But if you're the kind of parent that doesn't follow through on threats, she'll probably blow you off and not study."

"Everything you've just shared with me relates to the old strategies of influencing teens. And you're right, the situation does depend on a lot of factors, most of which you, as the parent, have little or no control over.

"The problem with the traditional strategy you just described is that even in the best-case scenario, one where the teen actually does study, the parent has done nothing more than provide a temporary solution to a long-term problem.

"For instance, if the teen no longer considers the consequences harmful, or if the parent is not around to enforce the consequences, how long do you think this teen would continue to study without a reminder?"

"Probably not long," Greg admitted.

"And that's in the best-case scenario. So, let's back up for a moment. Given the situation, what would be the ideal outcome for this teen?"

After reflecting a moment, Greg replied, "To take studying more seriously, and to continue to study without being reminded by her parents—for her to be self-motivated."

"You're absolutely right. Now let me show you how coaching a teen is different from parenting one. Parent coaches know that in order to motivate their children to do anything, they must first understand the motives behind their children's behavior. *Motive* is the root word of motivate. Motives are the reasons for anything and everything we do. Instead of focusing on getting this teen to study, parent coaches would try to find out *why* this teen doesn't want to study in the first place. By uncovering the motives, you can discover what truly motivates your teen."

Greg looked thoughtful. Vince finished his coffee and asked, "What do you think?"

Greg paused and then said, "Vince, this hasn't been entirely fun, but it has been helpful. After I have a chance to think this over and try using the things we talked about, could we meet again?"

Vince replied, "I would be happy to meet again. I've enjoyed meeting you as well as our discussion. And I think I can be of some help. If you are up to it, let's plan on meeting several more times over the next few months, so that I can help you better understand how this process works."

"Process?" Greg asked, confused.

"Yes, this is a process," Vince said. "And it can be a frustrating one. As you make progress with your teen, setbacks—such as arguments, breaking rules, or not studying—might begin to seem more and more difficult to handle. So let me say at the outset that this process is gradual. You'll most likely find yourself taking three steps forward, then two steps back. But through it all I think you will come to better understand your teen's motives and how to use them to help her become self-motivated, while improving your relationship in the process. Isn't that what you're hoping to achieve?"

"I guess so. But I just don't believe that's possible. You don't know my daughter; she's a tough egg to crack. I've tried almost everything, but with no success."

"Remember what I told you, Greg," Vince said calmly. "In order to change anything, you have to first change your own attitude about it. Anything is possible. And if you haven't tried being more of a coach than a parent to Kelly, then you haven't tried everything. I'm not going to show you how to 'crack' your daughter, but I'll share with you ideas that can help you get your daughter to dismantle her own shell, so that you can look inside. Remember that true motivation comes from within. You have to help your daughter find it . . . *on her own.* Not only will this require listening on your part, but a lot of patience as well. But first you have to make a shift attitudinally yourself.

"Coaching techniques are not guaranteed. Every teen is different, and some strategies will work better than others. Keep doing what works, and stop doing what doesn't. All I can do is offer you a different perspective and a new approach. And don't worry—you won't be alone. I know you have a very supportive wife, and I'll make myself available to help you through this process—answer your questions, provide you feedback, help you to help your daughter and yourself.

"But here is the big question: Are you willing to do the personal work this will require?"

"I don't have a choice," Greg said, remembering not only the commitment he made to Kathy, but also, more important, the fact that he wanted a relationship, a good one, with his daughter, one that would provide a strong foundation for the rest of their lives. "What's the first step?"

"We've already completed the first step, which is to acknowledge that there is a problem, and change your thinking about parenting. I think we covered a lot of ground today and I suspect you need to think about what we discussed."

"Vince, I appreciate the time you spent with me. Can we meet again next week—same time, same place?"

"I would enjoy that," Vince replied as he extended his hand to Greg.

As Greg shook Vince's hand, he could feel his original resistance shifting to a more open, receptive outlook.

*   *   *

When Greg arrived home that evening and walked into the house, he found Kathy seated at the kitchen table, a pencil in one hand, a large pile of work spread out before her. She looked up and smiled. "Learn anything useful?" she asked.

Greg felt exhausted but energized. His meeting with Vince had brought out some difficult realities that he knew were important to face. But he was excited and hopeful. In a strange way, it all seemed like it might already be starting to come more easily for him.

"I did," he said. "I learned a lot."

What to Remember

- *Change your parenting strategy by thinking more like a coach than a parent.*

- *Ask yourself what kind of problem your teen is having with you.*

- *Listen to your teen in an effort to help her help herself.*

- *Feelings of anger—especially those of being misunderstood—are totally normal for both teenagers and parents.*

- *Acknowledge that you can improve as a parent.*

3

Being Courageous

September 27

I'm tired of being treated like a kid! Billy gets treated like more of an adult than I do. "Billy does what he's supposed to do," they say. Ha! He's got a whole stash of firecrackers out in the tool shed they don't even know about. He smokes with his friends. How perfect would he be if they knew that? I'm older, so I should get more independence. But they're always like where are you going and who's going to be there and when will you be home? Like the other night when Eric had a party because his parents were out of town. I had to say that I was staying at Tina's (which I did) and that we were going to the movies until 10 (which we didn't). But it was the only way to get to go to the party. I just wanted to see if Jeremy would be there because I heard he maybe wanted to ask me to homecoming. I don't care about what the kids are doing in the bathrooms or the upstairs rooms. But I can't even *explain that because it's like if I even admit that I know kids who do bad stuff then maybe I'll get grounded. It's totally unfair—turning the house into a prison. I hate feeling like I have to lie, but I need to have a life too! I feel like if I'm totally honest about what it's like to be a kid today, then they'll want to send me off to become a nun. They are so totally overprotective. It's not fair. I should be able to tell them what some of the other kids are like, and what I'm like. They'd probably have a lot less to worry about . . .*

*   *   *

A few weeks later, as Greg walked toward Starbuck's, he didn't quite feel the same anticipation and open-mindedness he'd felt after first meeting Vince. As he opened the door and went in, he wondered if he should be doing this. Slumping down in a chair he said, "Hey Vince, how are you?"

"I'm good," Vince replied. "And you?" Greg shrugged.

Vince rubbed his hands together and said, "So, Greg. Tell me. How did this last week go?"

Greg sighed, fingering a piece of lint stuck on his cuff. "All right," he said, thinking of the tantrum his son Billy had thrown about time limits on his playing video games, just as Greg was on his way out the door.

"Just all right?"

"Just all right, Vince. I wish I could say it was better." Greg leaned forward. "You were right about me needing to change my attitude about parenting, and my wife and I have had some really good conversations about how we can both do that. But the house is still almost unbearable. My daughter and I can barely manage to coexist. We've stopped yelling so much, but we still argue. And her younger brother seems to be picking up on some of this. He's gotten a sharp tongue and attitude, and taken to locking himself in his room when he doesn't get his way. At least with Kelly I know why we're yelling, but Billy just blows up for no reason and storms off to spend an unhealthy amount of time on the computer. He's totally noncommunicative. Always has been, I guess. But the outbursts are getting more and more frequent. I swear, I don't think I could handle two of them."

"Then that's the good news," Vince said. "You're not going to 'handle' either of them. You're going to *coach* them, as needed, based on who they are as individuals."

"I know, I know. And I really do believe that if we could get Kelly's attitude and behavior to improve, that her brother's might follow suit. But in addition to what my wife and I do, Kelly needs to change her attitude as well."

"Give me an example of that."

"Well," Greg began, leaning back in his seat. "Just last week I found a bunch of work applications Kelly was supposed to fill out lying in the trash—including two from restaurants that she said would definitely hire her! I was livid, but rather than yelling, I decided to try some of the strategies you discussed with me in our first meeting. I reminded her that she wanted a car when she turned sixteen, and that working was the way to save her portion of the money. I reminded her that her goal in wanting that car was freedom, and that proving herself responsible would earn her that freedom. But she just blew up at me! 'You don't care,' she said. 'You just want to push me around and tell me what to do.' I hate to say it, Vince, but it almost seems like I'm damned if I do and I'm damned if I don't."

Vince gave an understanding smile, and Greg flashed a quick look of shame and hurt.

"I don't mean to make light of the situation," Vince said, "but it's just another of those conflicts that parents are telling me about all the time."

"I know, I know. My daughter is totally normal."

"Your daughter *is* totally normal," Vince said. He looked at Greg, then continued. "What do you think set her off? Why such an explosive reaction to gentle reminders of her goals?"

"Well," Greg began, "I'm not sure. Maybe it's because I've told her over and over again that *I* saved to buy a car when I was sixteen."

"Good. What else?"

"What else? Maybe that I'm always reminding her that *I* got a job when I was fifteen, and more or less haven't been out of work ever since. And maybe I did overreact a little.

"I've got a lot of my own job stress right now. I've been passed over for promotion twice, and there's talk of additional cutbacks coming at the beginning of the year. It'd just be nice if she could occasionally treat herself to a movie . . . you know? Sometimes I feel like I'm supposed to be an ATM full of twenty-dollar bills."

"Good. Your honesty is admirable, Greg. Is there anything else?"

"Well, sometimes I get the feeling that she resents me for my successes."

"Resents you? In what way?"

"I guess . . . It's just that I think she feels a lot of pressure from me. Maybe I wasn't being such a great coach after all."

"You're being a fine coach, Greg. You're new to this game, and any coach in the world will tell you that practice makes perfect. But I do think you've hit on something here—the fact that your teen feels pressured by you."

"How else am I supposed to motivate her to get a job?" Greg said, exasperated.

"Remember, Greg, it's Kelly, not you, who has the fundamental responsibility for motivation. Only she can do that. What's really the problem here? Why is it so important that she get a job?"

Greg reflected silently for a moment. "Because I don't want her to fail," he said.

"That's right!" Vince told him, once again smiling. "And there's absolutely nothing wrong with that. You want the best for your teen; all parents do. Unfortunately, if desires for our children to succeed become too intense, that can often lead parents to place their own anxieties on their children. I call these anxieties 'parent fears,' and you've already identified one of them. In my work with parents, I have found the three most common fears are:

1. "The fear of their teen having to struggle, or to make similar 'life' mistakes.

2. "The fear that their teen will become dependent on them, or others, in order to survive.

3. "The fear that their children will not succeed in life, and that they—the parent—will be blamed for it.

"Does any of this sound familiar?"

"It sure does," Greg said. "But what's wrong with that? I try to respect her space, but getting a job is essential—it will help teach her to succeed. We all want our children to be better off than we were."

"There's nothing wrong with that feeling, Greg. What's wrong is that sometimes parents let these fears dominate the quality of their relationship with their teenager. And let's face it, these are fears that most teens couldn't care less about.

"So what are we left with?" Greg asked glumly. "A big, random universe where some kids succeed and others don't, and parents can't do a thing about it?"

"Of course not," Vince said. "Think about what you just said to me. 'A random universe where some kids succeed and others don't, and parents can't do a thing about it.' Does that sound logical to you?"

"No."

"Does it sound—not to insult you—kind of irrational?"

"Yes."

"All parents have these fears. You were right: All parents want more for their children than they had for themselves. And frankly with the incredible competition for good schools and jobs that we see in these times, we worry more for our children's futures. While it may be true that today is the first day of the rest of our lives, it is absolutely irrational to think that all is lost if our children wait until tomorrow."

"So what do I do in the meantime? I'm afraid that my daughter is going nowhere and it's all my fault."

"While that may not be rational either, it is good that you've said that. Once you understand that your fears are common, and that they're also irrational, the first step is to identify the fear. Let me ask you, Greg, of the three major fears I listed for you earlier, which sounds most likely for you?"

"Well, I guess it would be the third one. That I'm afraid if my teen doesn't succeed in life I'll be blamed for it."

"Exactly."

"So what do we do about it?"

"Let me ask you some questions. First of all, in terms of your work, do you want to be successful?"

"Of course. We all do."

"And who determines whether or not you're a successful worker?"

"Well, I guess my boss."

"So," Vince said, "if your boss thought you were successful, but in reality you were unqualified, unskilled, and incompetent—would you feel successful?"

Greg frowned. "Probably not."

"And given that, do you think your employer—or even your colleagues—are the best way to evaluate your worth and contribution to your job?"

"I guess not," Greg responded. "What difference would it make if my peers thought I was successful, when in reality I felt like a failure?"

"None. So what is it that would make you feel like a successful worker?"

Greg responded without hesitating. "If I take pride in my work and love what I do, and at the end of the day I know I've put in my best effort, then I'll know in my heart that I'm successful."

"What if *you* felt successful—confident, passionate, dedicated—but your colleagues thought you were a lousy employee?"

"Well, it really wouldn't matter what they thought; the only thing that would matter is how I felt about myself."

"Now we're getting somewhere, Greg. Let me ask you this: Do you want to be a successful parent?"

"Of course I do!"

Pointing a pencil as if to outline a play, Vince said, "Do your friends, the public, other parents, and the media determine if you're a successful parent?"

"No," Greg said, scratching his palm. "Not really."

"Ahh!" Vince said. "Then who would determine your success as a parent?"

"I guess I would. And to an extent, my daughter's opinion of me would play a part."

Vince grinned. "Then why do you think the biggest parent fear is that others will think we failed as a parent?"

"Because," Greg said firmly, "if your child fails, then that's a direct reflection on you as a parent."

"So what if a child succeeded in life, but his or her parents were emotionally and physically abusive? Would that mean that the child's parents were successful in rearing them?"

"Of course not!"

"Do you see what I'm getting at here?" Vince asked.

"I hate to seem cynical," Greg said, "but it sounds like we're back where we started. That some kids succeed, and others don't, and parents can't do a thing about it."

"Okay. Let's not take a step backward. We've already taken the first step and identified your fear. You may not have realized it, but we've been working through the second step, which is to move into and evaluate the fear."

"So the point of your questioning is that the fear is irrational?"

"Of course it is. As with any job, no one can make you feel like a failure without your consent. Think of the ways we try to teach our teenagers that they shouldn't allow others to determine how they feel about themselves—which is all too often the case with peer pressure. Now apply that same sense of independence to the way you think about yourself as a parent. No one else should be doing it for you. Instead of setting a goal of parent perfection—which is an impossible goal because we're only human, after all—we need to set a realistic goal. A simple goal. Something we've all been taught since birth. When all is said and done, the most important thing is to be able to look yourself in the mirror and say, 'I did my best.' Only you and your child will be able to honestly answer whether this is true."

"I've honestly tried to do my best, Vince. But if you asked Kelly today, I'm sure she'd say I've failed."

"Nonsense," Vince said. "You're talking to me, aren't you? It's important to realize that the appearance of success is not the same as being a success. If your daughter loved you plainly and openly, and told the world every chance she got, but it was only because you let her stay out till midnight and didn't have consequences for her cutting class, would you be a success?"

"No. I'm beginning to see what you mean more and more."

"Remember what I said? That no one can make you feel like a failure without your consent? This may even apply to your daughter sometimes. Since you get what you focus on in life, rather than focusing on failing as a parent, try to focus on succeeding as one. If you try to focus on becoming the kind of parent both *you* and your teen can be proud of, then you won't have time to worry about what others think."

"I see what you mean. Even when Kelly's angry with me, if I know I can be proud of my actions as a parent— proud to know I'm doing what I can to *help* her—then I'm working toward being a success."

"Exactly, Greg. You've made some real strides here today. First, you identified your fear. Then we stepped into and evaluated it. Do you think you're ready for the final step in this process?"

"What's that?"

"The third step is to move through the fear."

"How am I supposed to do that? Even if I see that it's irrational to fear someone else's criticisms of me for my daughter's actions, what can I do about it, so long as I'm feeling it?"

"Just like an employee who knows he's earned his paycheck, your fear will evaporate once you know—on the inside—that the fear is unfounded. Do you see what I'm saying?"

"That by being the kind of parent I want to be, my fear will evaporate?"

"Exactly."

"And how do I do that?"

"Greg, I'd like to give you an assignment for our next meeting. Would that be okay with you?"

"Sure, Vince."

"Good. Over the next week, I'd like you to complete the following steps:

1. "Write down three adjectives you would like your teenager to use in describing you as a parent.

2. "Under each of those adjectives, list the reasons why it is important to you.

3. "Evaluate where you are now as a parent: Are you moving closer to or farther away from the adjectives you listed in Step 1? (Hint: If you're standing still, you're moving farther away.)

4. "Make a list of the things you can do to move even closer to the kind of parent you described in Step 1.

5. "Make a commitment to do one thing a week from the list you made in Step 4.

"I know this may seem like a lot, but if you follow these steps—whether your daughter reacts noticeably or not—you will *feel* like a more successful parent."

"Well, I'll give it a try. Vince, after seeing how the next couple of weeks go, can I give you a call to schedule another time to meet?"

"That sounds good, Greg. I'll look forward to hearing from you."

"You got it. Thanks again."

With that the men shook hands and Greg walked off.

* * *

As Greg pulled into the driveway he saw Kathy on the front porch, where she had just hung up the phone with her mother.

"Mom says hi," Kathy said.

"How's she doing?" he asked.

"Fine. She had her five-year cancer checkup and the results were great. There weren't any signs of problems," Kathy reported, relieved.

"Thank God," Greg said, his mind shifting from thoughts of his assignment to his annual checkup, which he would somehow have to squeeze in.

"How was your meeting with Vince today?" Kathy asked.

"Good," Greg told her. "He shared some really terrific insights, like helping me identify my fears as a parent. For me, it's that Kelly's failures reflect poorly on us. He helped me understand that all parents have similar fears, and that they're irrational." Pausing, he sat next to Kathy and put his arm around her. "He also gave me an exercise to help ease these fears."

"Exercise? Like something that will help us show Kelly how to be more productive in her life?"

"Not exactly," Greg said. "More like something that can help us be the kind of parents we want to be, so that we know we've given Kelly what she needs."

"Do you think it will work?"

"I think it might. I'll tell you one thing, stranger or not, Vince is pretty easy to talk to. Thanks for having me try this."

"You're welcome," Kathy said. "I'm proud of you. I'm proud of you for being open to try something like this and then following through."

What to Remember

- *All parents have irrational fears—the best way to help your teen is to work through and eliminate these fears. Identify each fear, evaluate it, and move through it.*

- *Focus on succeeding as a parent. You determine your own parental success.*

Dealing with Real Life

December 8

I'm so mad at all of them. This has been the worst week of my life! If it's not bad enough that I failed the bio test I studied all night for, Mom and Dad decided I can't go skiing with Tina's family this weekend because of it. And no Internet except for school. They just don't want me to have a life. So now I can't even take a break and email my friends or check out what my favorite music groups are doing. Whatever! At least I got back at them when all I said was "I know" to everything they said and then gave them the "talk to the hand" gesture. And to top it off after all of that, I find out my stupid little brother threw his soccer jersey in with a load of my whites right as my back was turned—and now I've got a whole bunch of pinks to deal with. It's no wonder they don't understand when you stop to think about the way they dress—how embarrassing! I'm starting to think I'd be better off as an orphan. God, I hate this family! Okay, that's not true. After all, Mom did get up in the middle of the night to make some coffee for me when I was studying. But what the heck? She saw how hard I worked and now I'm punished anyway! And nothing happened to Billy. He ruined a whole load of my clothes and all they told him was to "be more aware" of what he was doing. They said it was different because it wasn't intentional. Screw that. Do they think I failed the test intentionally? He should be grounded this weekend too. At least I still get to go to the football game. Maybe the weekend won't be a total waste after all.

*   *   *

Greg's ears were ringing as he raced downtown, as if the phone mounted to his kitchen wall were sitting next to him on the seat. He could still hear the voice on the other end, could still feel the tightness in his chest that began the moment the voice said: "We found your daughter Kelly drinking in the school's parking lot. We'd like you to come down immediately."

A thousand thoughts sped through Greg's mind. Where did she get the alcohol? Had she done this before? Why at the school? He thought of all the progress they'd made over the past months. The math test he'd helped her study for—at her own request. The evening he and Kathy had come home to a surprise dinner cooked by Kelly. That never would have happened a few months earlier. Behaviors like these had given Greg a great deal of confidence in the strategies he was learning from Vince. On the other hand, there had been setbacks as well. Greg thought of the night Kelly came home two hours after curfew, explaining that she *deserved* to stay out late because she was with an older boy. When something like this happened, Greg worried that Kelly had no judgment or, worse, was slipping down the wrong path.

He thought of the weekly interruptions in his sleep and everyone else's, when Kelly would blast her stereo in the middle of the night. He thought of the clothes strewn about the house, piled on the stairs and in the corners, forever forgotten by Kelly. But those infractions were nothing compared to being caught drinking at school. Over and over Greg thought, "What kind of punishment will help her learn from this?"

With this in mind he walked up the steps to his daughter's school and into the main office.

"Mr. Giovanni?" the receptionist asked.

"Yes," he told her, fearing he may have detected a tone of disgust in her voice.

"The principal is waiting for you."

Behind the receptionist's desk he could see an open door, and through that the back of his daughter's head, her eyes obviously trained on the ground. Again he thought, "What kind of punishment will help her learn from this?"

This thought stayed in his mind for the entire 20 minutes. He shifted uncomfortably in the seat next to Kelly. He listened to the principal recount how school officials found his daughter drinking beer. It stayed with him as the principal went on to explain that a 12-pack had been found mostly empty, that Kelly and her best friend Tina had been found intoxicated, and that they had apparently snuck off from the football game to drink in a friend's car.

Greg continued to shift uncomfortably as the principal laid out the school's Code of Conduct. A zero-tolerance policy was in effect for alcohol, drugs, and smoking. Kelly and her friend Tina would be immediately suspended for one week, and Kelly's involvement in the theater program suspended until the following school year. Greg again felt the tightness in his chest. And he felt angry.

The anger caused him to pull on his daughter's arm as he led her out of the school. Not to hurt her. Never. Just to scare her. Greg thought it only fair that she know how scared he had been for the past hour.

As they sat in the car, a silence loomed between them. It was Greg who finally let out a cough and broke the silence. "So what do you have to say for yourself, Kelly?"

Kelly just stared straight ahead.

"Would you like to tell me why you thought boozing it up at school *of all places* was a smart thing to do?"

"I guess it wasn't so smart," she finally said.

"You're darn right it wasn't smart!" Greg fumed. "Want to tell me where you got it, then?"

Again he was met with a chilly silence. Greg shook his head, then started the car and pulled out into traffic.

After a few moments, he finally said, "Fine. Then let me tell you why *I'm* so upset." He looked over at his daughter once, then returned his eyes to the road. "Don't you know that I have to work with the principal's husband at my office? And her receptionist. You know that she lives right next door to Bob Huntington, who Mom *works* with. Monday morning everyone's going to know that my daughter's a boozehound! How is this supposed to look to other people, Kelly? I can't believe you would humiliate me like this!"

"It was just a stupid football game," Kelly spat.

"And you're just a stupid child!" Greg roared. His temper was once again getting the best of him, but he had to make her *see* that her behavior was not at all okay. "You have no idea how disappointed your mother and I are. Where's the trust gone in this family, Kelly?"

She continued to sit motionless, giving no response.

"I'll tell you one thing: You're never hanging around with that Tina again!"

"But Dad," Kelly wailed, "she's my best friend."

"Best friend or not, she's a bad influence. Your mother and I have never liked that girl." This much was true. Greg and Kathy had agonized over the friendship from the very first, when the two girls had gotten together one day after school and dyed each other's hair red. Greg and Kathy felt that Tina's family was too permissive with money, boundaries, and excessive experiences. The old saying seemed to be true: Give them an inch, and they'll take a mile. "And now that they won't have you in theater," Greg continued, "you have no excuse for not getting a job."

Kelly started crying quietly, little sobs rolling through her shoulders.

"That'll be it for you," Greg said. "To school and work, and then home. No phone calls. No TV. No Internet. Just you alone in your room thinking about what you've done." Greg made a sharp left, then continued. "Your mother is absolutely crushed. She'll be ashamed to be seen at the company Christmas party this year, if I can even get her to go. Oh, wouldn't that be great! A misfit daughter and a wife who's afraid to be seen in public because of her." Greg sighed loudly—his daughter *would* come to understand what she'd done to her family.

"You don't care, you hypocrite!" Kelly yelled. "Maybe if you were a better father, I wouldn't have been drinking. Isn't that what you're scared your friends will think? You drink!" she screamed.

"Enough!" Greg hollered, and as his daughter burst into loud sobs, he knew he would have preferred the silence.

As Greg crept the car into the garage, he looked over at his daughter's tear-soaked face, mascara streaming down her cheeks. "I want you to wipe off those tears and go straight to bed," Greg told her. "No one here feels sorry for you."

As Kelly pulled on the door handle and exited the car, she sighed under her breath. "I think I'm gonna be sick," she said.

Greg already was.

What to Remember

- *All teens make mistakes. Let your child know that good kids make bad decisions. You may be disappointed in her actions, but you believe in her as your daughter.*

- *What may at first seem like the end of the world is just one misstep in your child's process of becoming a responsible adult. Treat your teen as the adult she or he is becoming, and not as the prisoner of a mistake.*

- *Rarely is the "mistake" as bad as it seems at the outset to parents.*

THE OPPORTUNITY

Seeing a Different Outcome

December 9

Oh my God! I hate my father. Or he hates me. Last night Tina and I got caught drinking in the parking lot at school and he went nuts! All he cared about was what other people were going to think of him. Your mother and I this, and the neighbors will think that. It's like he thinks the whole world revolves around him. He doesn't even feel bad that I'm kicked out of theater! It's like he expects me to be perfect. Everybody makes mistakes. He is so not perfect himself. Last week, he came home from the office holiday party completely looped. He just doesn't understand. Plain and simple. I could be out doing drugs and sleeping with the entire football team, and instead I'm getting mostly good grades and working hard on makeup and costumes for the next play. A couple of beers and it's like the world ended. High school is so hard. It's like you have to look this way to fit in, and weigh that much to be pretty. There's so much pressure from teachers to act a certain way, and my math and science classes are really hard. So what if I drank some beer? He drinks! Hypocrite. I wish he could just live inside my head for one day so that he could see how hard high school is, and how easy it would be for me to go out and do bad stuff all the time. But I don't. He should be proud. I know I made a mistake. But isn't that how we learn? Isn't that what adults are always telling us? At least Mom was a little cooler. She let me know she was upset and disappointed but at least she didn't lecture me like Dad. And that hangover. Ugh! Did my head hurt this morning! I don't think I'm going to drink any more for a long, long time. But I don't think I'm going to tell Dad that.

*   *   *

reg's nostrils flared as he anxiously waited for Vince. True, he always tried to put his best foot forward, but things were getting out of hand. His daughter caught drinking at school! Then her defiance of Greg's punishment by leaving the house the next day for some supposed job hunting, only to return without a single application. "Probably out with that Tina," Greg thought.

But at least he was able to schedule an emergency meeting with Vince. Greg realized that Vince was doing him a great favor, meeting him unscheduled like this, and he made a mental note to calm himself. He blew on the cup of coffee he was holding, then took a small sip.

When Vince walked through the door, the clerk behind the counter asked, "Get you the usual, Vince?" He waved and said, "Yeah, thanks, Todd." Then he took off his coat and sat down across from Greg. "So . . . to what do we owe this surprise meeting?"

Greg leaned forward and braced himself. "Kelly was found drinking on school grounds."

Vince caught Greg's eyes and nodded sympathetically. "Teens do tend to create trouble for themselves," he said.

"You're preaching to the choir," Greg told him.

"Why don't you tell me what happened?" Vince asked.

Greg recounted all the gory details. The phone call. The curt receptionist. His daughter's removal from the theater troupe. His own outburst in the car, his daughter's crying, and of course, her refusal to accept the consequences. He also shared his extreme frustration over allowing himself to get caught up in the heat of the moment.

"But I just don't know how I can make her listen!" Greg finally ended.

"Remember, Greg," Vince said, sipping the coffee the clerk had just set down on the table. "You can't *make* anyone else do anything. But let's get back to that later. For the time being," he went on, "I want to help you evaluate this situation. I have some questions I want to ask you."

Greg took a deep breath. "Okay, I'm ready when you are."

"First off: What did you do right in this situation?"

Greg did not hesitate. "I let her know that what she did was wrong. That our actions have consequences. I let her know that she hurt her family, and that she'd be punished."

"That's good. Those are all perfectly fine responses. Now let me ask you this: What did you do wrong in this situation?"

Greg put his hands on the edge of the table and let out a sigh before beginning. "Well, I'm worried I may have done a lot wrong, actually. I've been turning it over in my head and I think I made some bad choices."

"That's okay, Greg. You're still learning. And try not to doubt yourself. Tell me what you did wrong."

"Well, I yelled a lot. Enough to make Kelly cry. And I responded to her sarcasm with biting remarks. I let her bait me . . ." Greg trailed off.

"What else?"

"I scolded her for all the ways this situation will affect me, never thinking how it might feel to be kicked out of theater. And I . . . I . . ."

"Go ahead," Vince told him.

"Part of her punishment was that I forbid her to see the friend she was caught with."

"And you think that's something you did wrong?"

"Won't it just make Kelly want to hang around her more?"

"Probably," Vince said, smiling. "And it gives her an ally. It's now them versus you."

Greg rolled his eyes. "Great!"

"The good news is, more has been gained here than lost. Consider this: What did you really fear? In other words: Why did you really react the way you did?"

"Other than feeling humiliated?" Greg asked.

"Talk about that."

"About being humiliated? Well, my wife and I know a lot of people involved at the school, we work with some of their spouses, and now everyone will think we're bad parents. I guess that's why I came down on her so hard."

"Do you feel you made this situation all about yourself?"

"But it is about me!" Greg said. "And my wife, and our family."

"It's also about Kelly," Vince reminded him. "Happy people don't often act this way. Does that give her an excuse? Of course not. Remember, though, your success as a parent isn't measured by anyone else."

"I know."

"How do you feel as a parent right now?"

"Lousy. Now all of our friends and colleagues will know we can't control our daughter."

"They can't control theirs either," Vince told him. "And that's not why you're here."

"I know, I know," Greg said. "I'm here to find ways to *help* Kelly."

"Exactly!"

"And I can't motivate her, but I can help her motivate herself."

"You're learning."

"And you're right. I determine my own success as a parent."

"And what do you fear most about this whole situation right now?"

Greg paused, clearing his throat uncomfortably. "That my daughter might be right for feeling angry toward me."

"What opportunities did you miss to build a bridge with your daughter?"

"To build a bridge? That's a tough one . . ." He paused in reflection. "I guess I could have been clearer that I was coming from a place of love."

"Explain what you mean by that."

"I could have been firm without blowing up. I could have helped her look at her decision, and how it would affect her, rather than reminding her of all the ways it affected me."

"What else?"

"I could have presented her need to get a job as a way to learn from her mistake, rather than as a punishment."

"That's very true. Anything more?"

"I guess I should have let her know that her mother and I love her no matter what, and that we'd get through this together."

"See? You're figuring this all out on your own. And you're absolutely right. We can weather any problem as long as we're clear that there is a foundation of love for the relationship. No matter how mad you get, or how much you and Kelly disagree, you can both be comforted that the love that you share will allow you to work through these conflicts and sustain your relationship. What do you think would have happened if you had done more to keep this in mind?"

Greg shrugged. "Kelly might have responded more openly."

"What do you mean?"

"She won't even admit that what she did was wrong."

"So Greg, as with all of our lessons, let me finally ask you, what did you learn?"

"I guess I learned that Kelly's actions are her own, and that they affect her every bit as much as they do me— more so, probably. And that I should keep this in mind when I'm reacting to a rough situation."

"Good. All perfectly valid responses. But let's look at this more closely. Remember when we talked about most parents having the same fears and anxieties over their children?"

Greg nodded. "You used it to illustrate that my daughter is perfectly normal."

"That's right. What you may not have realized is that in talking to teens, I find across the board that they too list many of the same concerns about their parents."

"So are you about to tell me that I'm a completely normal father, or an abnormal psychopath?"

Vince laughed. "Neither, Greg. You're going to answer that for yourself. Think about this: Parents are programmed to react in certain ways to certain behaviors, in much the same way teens are programmed to rebel against authority. Let me list the biggest grievances teens have about their parents:

1. "That their parents make decisions for them.

2. "That they are too controlling.

3. "That they are overprotective.

4. "That parents try to live vicariously through them.

5. "That a parent's love sometimes feels conditional.

6. "That parents have unrealistic expectations, or that they expect perfection.

7. "That parents project their own fears and insecurities on their children.

8. "That parents don't practice what they preach.

"Does any of this seem to fit with what we were just talking about?"

"Yeah," Greg said, "it does. Pretty much all of it."

"I refer to attributes like these as 'success-sabotaging behavior.'"

"Great!" Greg said. "So now this is all my fault?" Once again, he was second-guessing himself.

"Of course not," Vince said. "Just as your teen is perfectly normal, these are all perfectly normal ways for parents to respond to the stress of raising a child. But we're not responding like parents anymore, Greg. We're trying to think like coaches."

Greg nodded.

"You already mentioned that making the job search a punishment caused your daughter to refuse, and that forbidding her to see her friend will only make her more likely to do so. Do you see what I mean by success-sabotaging behavior?"

"Yeah, I do. You mean that if I'd tried to *show* her what was wrong, rather than *tell* her, that she may have learned something from this?"

"You're on the right track, Greg. I've already asked you what you learned from this episode. Now let me ask this: What's the best possible thing you could have done to handle the situation better?"

"I could have tried to show Kelly that the worst of what she'd done was to hurt herself, and to let her know that I'd be there for her no matter what."

"Well, Greg," Vince said, smiling. "I think it's time for your next assignment."

"Go ahead."

"I want you to enact the solution you just proposed. Try to help Kelly understand that she's really hurting *herself,* and be sure to let her know that you'll always be there for her."

"I'll try. But that won't be easy. Sometimes she just gets under my skin so quickly. Like the other day. Kelly yelled at her mother when she found out we were not going out to have one of her favorite fast foods for dinner that night. Apparently she's too busy to do her hair, and her homework, and feed herself occasionally. And when Kathy or I cook, Kelly doesn't even pitch in with the dishes. Sometimes I'm just so full of doubt. Do I ignore it, or yell about it? I sometimes can't see the line between being too permissive and being too harsh."

"Let me share something with you, Greg. It's not your job to retaliate against your daughter's anger. What you need to do is *survive* in the face of her anger. You see, Greg, when you react to Kelly's rage by overly emphasizing your own, her ability to be self-assertive diminishes. She learns to put herself down, because she feels the outside world—you, Greg—doing the same."

"So now you're saying I've caused my daughter to have low self-esteem, too?"

"Not at all. What I'm saying is that if you learn to back away, even a little, your daughter will naturally start to feel that her anger toward you is too powerful. Believe it or not, Greg, she seeks your approval. All children feel a need for their parents' approval. By backing off from her anger, your daughter will eventually come to feel that she's driven you away—someone she loves and needs. Anger will seem less like a useful tool, and more like a harmful emotion."

"I can see how this is another way to help Kelly help herself."

"Exactly. You really are starting to think like a coach. So listen to this carefully: If there's one thing I want you to take away from our conversation today, it's that you can't expect to change others without first changing yourself."

"I think I understand," Greg said. "Thanks so much for meeting me unexpectedly like this."

"Of course," Vince told him. "And when you're feeling frustrated, I want you to always remember that this is a process. It may be that you've just taken a couple of steps back, but think of how many forward steps you've made in these last months."

"That's good advice, Vince. Thanks. I'll give you a call and let you know how things are going."

"I'll look forward to hearing from you."

"You will."

And with that the two shook hands and went their separate ways.

* * *

Later that evening, as they lay in bed, Greg told Kathy about his emergency meeting with Vince.

"What did he say that could help?" she asked.

"He helped me see that this problem has much more to do with Kelly than it does with you and me. He helped me see that Kelly needs our help, not indignation."

"And did he tell you how we can help her?"

"He told me that we can't change anyone else's behavior without first changing our own."

"So what are you going to do about it?" she asked, squeezing his hand.

Greg turned to look his wife in the eyes. "If she won't apologize for her behavior," he said, "then I'll apologize for mine."

What to Remember

- *Like your teen, you are responsible for your own behavior.*

- *Your teen is much more likely to "do as you do" than to "do as you say."*

- *Teens are quicker to respond to openness and love than to reproach and punishment.*

- *You can love the teen, separate from the action or judgment that was the "mistake." By separating the two, your teen learns that you love and believe in them even though, in their mistake, they made a bad decision.*

Breaking Through Barriers

December 10

Greg's letter read,

Dear Kelly,

My daughter. I still remember the day you were born. The proudest day of my life. I never told you this, but I believed I could see into the future that day. I saw my little girl growing up, saw her chasing fireflies at dusk, baking sugar cookies with her mother, learning to change the oil in the family car with her father. And we've seen all these things come true, you, your mother, and I.

But, Kelly, there were other things I know I didn't see that day. I didn't see the time you would fall out of the oak tree in the front yard and break your arm. I didn't know that your injury would hurt me more than when I'd broken my own arm. I didn't know on that day you joined us in this world that looking at your tears would make me want to cry myself. But they did. I knew I would love you, but until I became a father I'm not sure I knew what love meant.

There were other things I couldn't see on that day, too. I couldn't see MTV or rap or children with guns in their lockers at school. You've grown up in a world that I don't know, and your world frightens me. It takes away a young adult's right to innocence. Your world is faster than mine was. Harder. I think I have no choice but to admire the courage you have for facing such a strange place every day.

You've grown into an amazing young woman, Kelly. I think I can still see into the future, and now I see the absolutely incredible adult you will become. But I can also see into the past, and I'll never forget the little girl you were. And that's the little girl Daddy still tries to protect. So I apologize if I'm occasionally overzealous in that endeavor.

I can't protect you from yourself. I can't even try to stop you from making your own mistakes—how else will you learn? I don't blame myself for trying, though. I'm talking about the same feeling I had when you broke your arm, and all I wanted in the world was to go back in time and break your fall. Heck, I'd have taken that fall for you, if I could.

But, Kelly, there is something I blame myself for. I haven't been there for you in the way you need me to be there. When you make your mistakes, it's not my job to point them out. I'm sorry I've done this. It's my job to help you learn from them.

So here are my apologies:

I apologize for the way I reacted when you were caught drinking at your school. Nothing I could have said could've possibly made you feel any worse than you were probably feeling already. I'm sorry for trying to add to that, rather than respecting your feelings, and discussing matters with you appropriately.

I apologize that I yelled at you. For this there is no excuse. I realize now that it's no different for me to yell at you, than it is for you to yell at me. Neither of us likes it, and I will try to do a better job of leading by example. We all have tempers, and I promise to do my very best to keep mine under control in the future.

I apologize for forbidding you to see your friend. If I'm willing to admit that we all make mistakes, and that mistakes are necessary for us to learn, then I can't blame your friend for your mistake. Sometimes you will learn on your own, and sometimes you will learn with others. I will love you no matter what.

Finally, I apologize for making the whole affair about myself. It was not at all about me, it was about you, and I let you down. The last thing that ever should have entered my mind was what others might think about your mother or me. The first thing that should have entered my mind was to ask if you were okay. I'm sorry I didn't ask you that, or why you had done this, or what I could do to help. If I had done these things, I can't help but think you and I would be speaking today.

I can't change the past, any more than you can erase this blunder. (Not that you need to, so long as you build from it.)

What I can do is change myself, and therefore change the future. I promise you, Kelly: I will listen more, and tell less. I will try harder to help, and even harder to stay out of your way as you make your own decisions. But I will be there, when those decisions are hard, to help you weigh consequences and focus on the future. I will treat you less like the little girl I can still see, and more like the woman you will become. Nothing is lost, Kelly. In you I see a budding adult who is full of confidence and self-awareness, who chooses right from wrong, and who loves those around her. And I will treat you with the respect you deserve for the person you are trying to become.

I'm downstairs now. I've just put a pot on to boil. I have your favorite—chamomile. If you'd like a cup of tea, please come down. I'd love to talk to my daughter again.

I love you more than anything in the whole world, and I miss you.

Love,

Dad

*   *   *

Greg froze when he heard the thumping of footsteps coming down the stairs. He knew it would be Kelly, but he just didn't know *how* she would respond. There'd been a lump in his throat when he slipped the letter under her door, so he hadn't said anything. "She'll either storm out of the house," he thought, "or come talk to me. Either way, I've done the best I can."

"Dad?"

Greg turned immediately when he heard the voice behind him. The first thing he noticed was his letter, hanging limply from Kelly's hand. Then his gaze moved up, and he saw a pair of puffy, tear-soaked eyes.

"Kelly?"

"I love you, Dad," she said.

"I love you, too."

Greg held his breath as he went to embrace his daughter, and when he felt her return his hug he breathed deeply and squeezed even tighter.

"You've got me so scared," he told her.

"I'm scared too," she said, and after a moment added: "And I'm sorry."

"I'm sorry too." A shudder ran through his shoulders. "I'm so sorry, Kelly."

The two stood there like that for a few minutes, feeling closer than they had in longer than either could remember.

Finally, Greg broke the embrace and said, "Do you want some tea?"

Kelly smiled and looked at him lovingly. "Sure."

They sat at the kitchen table and Greg poured boiling water into the cups he had already set out. Then he took his daughter's hand in his own and said, "I guess we've got some figuring out to do."

"Yeah," Kelly agreed. "I guess we do."

"You read my letter? Obviously."

"I read it." She paused, and eventually said, "I didn't know you loved me that much. I feel like a bad daughter."

"And I feel like a bad father," Greg said, laughing. "But don't ever doubt that I love you."

"I feel like, you know, if we'd talked sooner, then maybe this would never have happened?"

"I feel that way too."

"So . . . what do we do about it?"

"Well," Greg said, feeling more than a little relief, "we're talking now."

"So talk," Kelly said, blowing on her tea.

"I want you to know that you're not a bad daughter. You're an amazing kid!" He squeezed her hand as he said this. "I see so much potential in you. You're a talented English student. A caring person. Your work on the school plays is fantastic! And I've seen you make lots of great decisions, too.

"I've heard you talk about a life beyond this one now, one with possibilities of college and a career. I'm so proud to have a daughter who looks at the future like that, even when it probably seems so far away and even daunting right now. And I really am sorry for all those mistakes of mine that I mentioned in that letter."

"I'm sorry, too," Kelly chimed in. "I shouldn't have embarrassed you and Mom like that. I . . ."

"Shush," Greg interrupted. "That's okay. Making you feel guilty was *my* fault."

"And making you feel like you had to say that stuff was *my* fault. I don't know, like maybe you were really scared on your way to pick me up. You know?"

"I was," Greg said, hardly able to believe how intuitive his daughter had become.

"*I'd* be angry if someone made me really scared for no reason. I broke the rules when I knew better. I'm sorry I scared you and Mom. And I'm also sorry for embarrassing you like that."

"That's all right," Greg told her. "I accept your apology." He paused. "Do you accept mine?"

"Of course I do, Dad." She reached out to him across the table and gave him a big hug.

As they shifted their weight back into their seats, Greg went on. "The thing about being a kid—and I was one too, so don't get defensive—is that you're going to make mistakes. Lots of them. And that's okay. That's *normal.* I made some, your mother made some, and someday your brother will probably make a bunch of his own. That's part of becoming an adult. And part of being a parent—someone who's made those mistakes already—is that you don't want to see your child go through the same pain you already went through. You want so much to have learned *for* them. But I know you have to learn for yourself. That you have to experiment to find out who you are. How else will you become you? The adult you."

"Thanks, Dad," Kelly said. "I guess I never thought about it before, but some of this stuff's probably new for you, too. I guess you should get to make *some* mistakes."

Greg laughed. "You mean it's okay with you that your mother and I aren't perfect? Wait, wait . . . I need to get a tape recorder for this one."

Kelly joined his laughter and replied, "Don't make fun of me, Dad. I mean it."

"Thank you, Kelly. I guess maybe we're more alike sometimes than we really want to admit. I think it's important for us both to remember that one incident doesn't change everything. You're still my kid. You always will be.

"I think the important thing here is that we both learned a lesson. The only way for us to get ahead as a family is for us to work together, and concentrate on strong communication. The thing is, I really do love you no matter what, and we both need to keep in mind that our love for each other will get us through the toughest of times. I want you to know that I've learned a lot from this experience, and that I'm committed to working on being a better parent and a better person in the future."

"Dad," Kelly said, a tear coming to her eye, "I'll try to be a better daughter, too."

"I appreciate that," Greg told her. "Be you. Find yourself. Do your best to stay out of trouble, and have an open mind about the lessons that lie ahead—both positive and negative."

"And if I don't?" Kelly asked, smirking mischievously.

"Then I'll still love you the same and we'll work through it together. That's the important thing, Kelly: That we work through our problems together by communicating openly. This isn't the end. We'll have more snags in the future. But, if we know this now, and anticipate the problems, maybe we can do something about them ahead of time."

"Like what?"

"I think we should agree to take the high road. You know, to work through problems that arise in the most positive way we can. Look what we've just been through, Kelly. And look at where we are now—*right now*. No matter how much we yell and point fingers, we'll always end up right here. Sipping tea and valuing each other. We need to keep that in mind when problems come up. It'll save us both a lot of heartache."

"That's really smart thinking, Dad. What made you come up with all this?"

Greg paused, momentarily embarrassed, then realized he should be no more ashamed of the help he received from Vince than he should be of his own daughter. "Well," he began, "I'm afraid I can't take *all* the credit. I met this great guy, a smart man who likes to help parents work through stuff with their kids—you could call him a parenting coach—who helped me work through some of our family issues."

"Parenting coach?" Kelly asked.

Over the next few minutes Greg filled her in on his meetings with Vince, emphasizing that Vince never once laid the blame at Kelly's feet. "He knows we're both only human, after all," Greg concluded.

"What's Mom think about all this?"

"Actually, it was your mother who got me to go. And I'm thankful she did. She and I have been talking over all of my meetings with Vince, and she's trying to do a better job too." After pausing a moment to reflect, Greg asked: "Does that sound like something you'd be interested in? Either meeting this man, or someone else you could talk to?"

"I don't know," Kelly said hesitantly. "Let me think about it."

"It could help," Greg prodded.

"I'll think about it," Kelly said again.

As Greg opened his mouth, he almost bit down on his tongue. Was he really about to be indignant? To point out that help shouldn't be turned down lightly? Yes, he was. "I'm not going to be left second-guessing myself on this one," he thought, then said aloud: "Well, just know that it's there for you. If you want it."

*   *   *

Greg was five minutes early for his appointment with Vince. He was eager to tell him of his progress, albeit slow, with Kelly.

"How did it go this week?" Vince asked, and Greg recounted the week's events.

"Sounds like you are making progress," Vince replied. But I have one more place for you to look to improve your relationship with Kelly. We've mentioned it several times, but we've never discussed it directly. I call it 'getting caught in the act.'"

"Lay it on me," Greg said.

"To what extent do you model for Kelly the behavior you would like her to follow?"

"What do you mean?"

"Are your own actions exemplary of the characteristics you are trying to inspire in her? In other words, do you walk your walk or do you just talk the talk?"

Greg paused, deflated, before responding honestly, "I know that sometimes I drink too much around Kelly. Last week I had way too much to drink at our company party. She looked completely disgusted when I walked in the door."

"That is a perfect example," Vince said. "When you think about it further, there may be other actions or behaviors you can align. Teens need to catch their parents doing the things that parents ask them to do—catch you being consistent in your words and actions—so you cease to be a hypocrite in their minds.

"I hope I didn't burst your bubble today. I know that you are making a lot of progress with Kelly, but I felt if we didn't get this crucial item on the table, some of the good you've established could quickly unravel."

"I appreciate it. I'll do some soul-searching to see how I could 'walk the talk' better," Greg said.

"I want to acknowledge your tenacity in this process, Greg."

"Thanks for continuing to teach me what I really need to learn. At times I feel overwhelmed, but I know I'll get it."

"You will," Vince assured him.

What to Remember

- *Teens respond to anger by displaying anger. By backing off in the face of your teen's anger, you are more likely to establish open dialogue. Strong but timely communication is the key to improving any relationship.*

- *To earn respect, get caught in the behaviors you would like of your teen.* Walk the talk.

- *Follow through and deliver on your promises; children don't forget.*

- *Be open, honest, and respectful when communicating with your teen.*

Creating the Best Outcome

December 28

Okay. So Dad wrote me this really nice letter. It actually made me cry to realize how much he loves me. We had a talk and even though he was maybe a little overboard with all this love and respect stuff, I thought that maybe he finally realized that I've been trying really hard. We hugged and I felt really good. And things have been going pretty good for the past couple of weeks. But today, he was going through the bills, and he opened the cell phone bill, and (oops, I did it again!) the minutes went over. "You're 87 minutes over your package, young lady!" Big deal. What a jerk. What is that, like ten dollars anyway? I mean, we're finally getting along where I think that maybe I'll still speak to him after I move out, and then he blows up all over again. He didn't yell or anything, but he made me feel really bad. Like if there's one, tiny little thing you aren't quite responsible with then you can't possibly be responsible with anything. Look at how responsible he is with raising his daughter! He spewed all this nonsense about how when problems come up in the future we'd agree to look at them objectively, and show love and respect first and foremost with working through them. But that all flew out the window when Kelly went and used 87 extra minutes on the phone. Stupid me! But then again, I did put him through a lot with that whole mess down at school. I really would like to get along better with Dad. Maybe if he does something so I can really see that he's trying, then I'll try a little harder too. I don't know. Maybe he really was trying. I mean, he didn't yell at me after all.

*   *   *

That's good to hear," Vince said. "It sounds like you're really starting to connect with your daughter. By backing away from her anger, you helped defuse the situation and allowed progress to be made."

"It sure helped, Vince. But stuff keeps happening that tests my patience and how I should respond."

The two men were once again seated in Starbuck's, sipping fresh cups of coffee. Greg had just recounted the details of his reconciliation with Kelly: the letter, the conversation, the tears, and the hugs.

"It sounds to me," Vince told him, "like you're really starting to get the hang of this."

"Not so fast, Vince. Listen, Kelly's response to the letter was great and things have been much better for the last several weeks. But a couple of days ago, I opened an enormous cell phone bill, and kind of snapped something about her needing to be more responsible. I felt bad because it really had more to do with my own job stress than the few extra dollars the phone was costing me. It didn't turn into a major thing, but she did withdraw a little."

"Don't worry," Vince interrupted. "Sometimes that's the nature of working through problems with your kids. As we discussed—two steps forward and one step back. But that's still progress. It's no different from dealing with other challenges in life. This may seem simplistic, but think about this example: Let's say it's Sunday evening and your final chore for the week is to fix a cracked oil pan in your car. You get your tools, slide underneath, and make the repair. Say that in the process a bunch of oil leaks down onto the cement. Now your last chore for the week is to clean the oil stain off the driveway. But you're still closer to your goal than you were before you started."

"I see what you mean. Every situation in life—regardless of what it may be—lends itself to the possibility of setbacks, but those setbacks don't necessarily erase previous milestones."

"Exactly. And while we're on the topic, let me ask you how you would have liked to handle the cell phone incident better."

"Well . . ." Greg began. "I suppose I should have started by showing her the bill and asking her about it.

She probably would have owned up to it right away, and I probably wouldn't have gotten so hot. I think, too, that I should have given her a chance to redeem herself."

"Redeem herself?" Vince asked.

"Tell her it's no big deal, and then assign her some chores to work off the extra expense. Or, ask her for ideas of how she can deal with it in the future—keep track of the time, maybe. Anything would have been better than acting so frustrated with her. When I look back in my own mind I think I may have acted as if she'd done it to disobey me, rather than giving her the benefit of the doubt. After all, we all make mistakes."

"That's right. And you're just as entitled to the occasional mistake as she is. Look at it this way, Greg. You've reconnected with your daughter, and made her a promise. If you're sincere in your commitment to better parenting, your bond with your daughter will prove strong enough to take you anywhere! Remember the foundation of love that we talked about? Don't let a momentary lapse of judgment ruin your feelings about all you've accomplished so far."

"Thanks, Vince. Thanks for the vote of confidence."

"You earned it, Greg. And as you know, there's always more progress to be made, and there will always be setbacks to endure. We all are destined to make more mistakes, just as your daughter will."

"That's good advice," Greg said. Then Greg paused and shifted uncomfortably in his seat.

"Something wrong?"

Greg coughed, then leaned forward. "Well, Vince, there *is* something. It's not the same type of concern we've been talking about so far, but I'm not sure how to handle it."

"Tell me about it, Greg."

"It's like this: I recognize that I can't motivate my daughter. But I also know firsthand that the future sneaks up on all of us and becomes the past. How can I get her to take a more active interest in her future?"

Vince laughed. "So many concerns, so little time, eh? You already know the answers to this one. Look inside and tell me what you find."

Greg closed his eyes and reflected a minute. He thought back over his encounters with Vince, and was surprised to realize how much he had learned to think like a coach. He finally said, "I'm going to help my daughter motivate herself."

"Exactly! And how are you going to do that?"

Again Greg paused to reflect. "I'm going to ask her what she's interested in."

"And then . . .?"

"I'm going to listen. I'm going to *really, really* listen to what she has to say."

"And what if you don't like it?"

"I'm *going* to like it. Because she's my daughter. Her interest will become my interest."

"That's a good approach to take. And while we're on the topic, let's talk about why listening is so important here."

Greg didn't miss a beat. "Because otherwise, I'll miss what it is she wants, what it is that will make her happy."

"And tell me why that would be a mistake."

"Because if I try to force, or even encourage Kelly to take the wrong path, or some path I may think is the right one for her, I'll be setting her up for failure."

"Likely," Vince said. "Or at least setting her up for the kind of discouragement that leads people to start all over again."

"How do you mean?"

"Think about it this way: A father asks his daughter where she would like to go to college. The daughter responds that if she decides to go at all, it will likely be to some West Coast school—UCLA, for the sake of argument. Say she likes the film school. Imagine that to this, her father replies: 'UCLA? Nonsense! There's nothing but crazies in Los Angeles. You don't want to go there. Take *my* alma mater, for example. The University of Pennsylvania. Beautiful campus, some of the best and brightest in the country, and one of the top business schools. I'll pull some strings and get you into the college, then after graduation you can join the family business.' Tell me, Greg, under this set of circumstances, should this particular father feel confused when his daughter comes home for winter break her freshman year with failing grades?"

"No. The father should have anticipated that."

"Why's that?"

"Because he gave his daughter the exact opposite of everything she wanted. East Coast, instead of West.

Business, rather than the arts. The staunch, conservative Ivy League, as opposed to the more progressive type of school she'd identified."

"But surely," Vince said, "there's nothing wrong with a parent wanting the best for their child? He sent her to the Ivy League. He spent many times what she would have needed for the education she identified for herself. Maybe he even helped get her into the sorority her mother had belonged to in college. When we're handed the best, isn't it just plain arrogance to throw it away?"

"Now hold on a minute, Vince!" Greg responded. "This girl we're talking about wanted something completely different. She *told* her father what she wanted, and what it would take for her to succeed. It's arrogance on *his part* if he thinks his daughter's job is to provide an outlet for his own selfish way of living vicariously!"

"That's right, Greg," Vince told him. "I'm just playing devil's advocate here."

Greg smiled, realizing he'd allowed himself to be baited.

"Sorry about the test," Vince went on. "But I wanted to make sure you were sincere about listening. Wanting the best for a child is very admirable. However, giving them the best you can to help them reach their own self-directed goals is even more admirable."

"I agree," Greg responded.

"So go home and talk this out with your daughter. I think you know how to handle this on your own, Coach Greg."

Greg smiled as he stood to shake Vince's hand. "I do. I'll be in touch to let you know how things work out."

"Good luck, Greg," Vince said, smiling warmly.

*   *   *

That night after dinner, Greg got Kelly's attention and asked if he could talk to her in the den.

"Am I in trouble again?" she asked.

"Not at all. I just want to chat. You know, part of our new deal."

So the two crossed the front hall into the den, and each took a seat on the big plush couch in front of the fireplace. A bookcase stretched along the wall behind them, and in front of them, on either side of the fireplace, Greg had framed and mounted his and Kathy's degrees.

"So, Kelly, I wanted to talk to you about a couple of things."

"Okay."

"First off, I'm sorry I kind of snapped over that phone bill the other day. It wasn't necessary, and I apologize."

Kelly paused in thought for a moment, then said "That's okay, Dad. Make you a deal? I'll try to keep better track of my minutes, if you keep trying to work on your temper."

"Deal," Greg said, relieved.

"Anything else?" Kelly asked, already starting to rise from her seat.

"Actually, there is. What do you think you want to do with your life?"

Kelly sighed. "You know that I don't know yet. I mean, I'm just a kid."

"I understand," Greg said. "Let me rephrase that: What is your passion? What gets Kelly really excited?"

"Let me see . . ." she said, reflecting. "I guess I really like my English class. I like all the stories we read and the discussions afterward. I also really enjoy writing in my journal."

"Why is that? What is it about these activities that gets you so excited?"

Kelly shifted her weight, leaning in toward her father. "It's like life, you know. Reading stories about people. Writing stories about the people I meet. Finding the hidden meaning in things. You know."

"I didn't know," Greg said. "But I'm glad you're telling me about it. So let me ask you this: What kind of activities and professions relate to your passion?"

"Let's see . . ." Kelly said. "I guess I never really thought about that before. Hmm . . . I guess I could be a writer . . . or an English teacher . . . or maybe even some kind of historian? You know, like study old documents and stories and things."

"That's great, Kelly! Those are all fine careers. Some things that *I* thought of were that you could also be an editor, or a publisher. You could be a journalist, or even a screenwriter. The important thing about being passionate about something is that it makes every day enjoyable—opens so many doors for growth and enrichment."

"You know, I never really thought of it like that before, but I guess there are a lot of things out there I might enjoy. It's kind of overwhelming."

"That's all right," Greg said, chuckling. "You were right when we started this conversation: You've got lots of time to think about this. But in the meantime, we can do some thinking to get you closer. For example: Think of an individual who's somehow professionally involved in your passion."

"Well," Kelly said, "there's my English teacher, Mrs. Johnson. She really gets into discussing the stories we read, and helping us find the hidden meaning. She calls it the 'theme.' I think that's pretty cool. Then there's my favorite writer—Flannery O'Connor. She writes all these really terrific stories about the types of people and towns that she spent her life around. That seems pretty interesting. I don't know, maybe even being an editor for a great writer like that would be fun."

Greg was so proud he couldn't stand to hide it any longer, and reached out to pinch his daughter's cheek.

"Daaaaaad!" she said. "I'm not eight anymore."

"I know," Greg told her. "I'm sorry. Listen, you're really doing a good job of thinking about this stuff. Let me ask you something else. What do you think any of these people were like as a child, or a teenager, or even a college student?"

"That's tough," Kelly said. "I didn't know any of those people back then."

"Just try," Greg countered. "There's no right and wrong."

"Okay . . . Well, I guess they probably liked to read a lot."

"Mmm hmm."

"And they probably wrote. I mean, even an editor probably started out writing, so they could understand it."

"What else?"

"I don't know . . . they observed life, people?"

"Probably," Greg said. "Do you think they went to writing seminars? Camps? What about attending readings around town? Or joining a book club at the library?"

"Probably," Kelly said thoughtfully. "Or, at least some of that stuff."

"How do you think the parents and teachers of these people would have described them?"

"I don't know . . . smart, curious, enterprising?"

"C'mon. Try again."

"I don't know, Dad, really. I guess hard working, dedicated."

"Anything else?"

"Passionate?"

"You're halfway there, Kelly. The truth is, I don't know either. Would you like to find out more about these people, so you can understand how they got to where they were?"

"Yeah, I would. That might be interesting, you know."

Greg could hardly believe his excitement. *We might have found something we can work on together!* Now he was in a position to share some attractive opportunities without forcing decisions on her. "Tell you what," he said.

"How about this weekend, the two of us go down to the library and do some research. We'll find out all about this writer you like, how she broke into the business, how her editor broke into his. Would you like that?"

"That would be great, Dad! And it'll be fun to do it together."

"It will," Greg said. "And in the meantime, maybe you can convince your English teacher to have lunch with you? You could develop a list of interview questions and find out how she got into her profession."

"That's a good idea. I'll ask Mrs. Johnson tomorrow. Maybe I should think about the kinds of things I want to find out at the library, too. You know, brainstorm?"

"I couldn't have put it better myself. So it's a date, then? This Saturday?"

"It's a date," she said, rising from the couch. "But right now I'm tired, so good night, Dad." She leaned forward and kissed Greg on the cheek.

"Good night, Kelly."

After she'd made her way upstairs, Greg turned off the lights in the den and walked to the kitchen, where Kathy was finishing a PowerPoint presentation she was to give the following morning.

"What'd you two talk about?" she asked.

"Kelly's future," Greg said proudly.

"You mean that you got our teenage daughter to admit there's a future beyond boys and shopping malls?"

Greg laughed. "I kind of tricked her," he said.

"How's that?"

"I asked her about her passion. She's really interested in English and writing. We're going to the library this weekend to do some research on the subject."

"No way," Kathy said. "Uh uh. You're the one getting all of Kelly's praise lately. I want a chance to do something for her."

"I think she'd like that. I'll tell her in the morning that you're going to take her." Kathy smiled, and Greg went on. "I was also thinking you could contact some local professionals in the field. Maybe writing and English professors at the college? Or someone who runs some kind of workshop? I was thinking you could set up an informal interview."

"Won't Kelly think of that as going behind her back? I think we should let her do that on her own, so we don't become parents who rescue their kids from their own learning process."

"You're right. Let's let her lead the way and let us know how we can help. I think she'll be thankful for our *help,* for our *involvement* in her passion."

"So what do we do once she sets up these interviews?"

"We'll get Kelly to develop a list of questions to ask the person. That way, she'll get the most out of the meeting, and maybe even find some new direction. She can practice on us and then go conduct them solo."

"You didn't used to be the kind of father who thought this way. So optimistic!"

"I didn't used to be the kind of father who knew how to coach," Greg said. "I want to help Kelly find her own way, by being encouraging and supportive, and by providing resources."

"And when she strikes off down her own path, won't you feel like you've lost your little girl?"

"No," Greg said, "I won't. I'll feel like I've gained a grown one."

What to Remember

- *Seek to connect with your child's passions, dreams, and goals. Successful parenting requires that you help your child achieve her own objectives, rather than create objectives for her.*

- *The only way to know your teen's goals and objectives is to ask, and then to really listen to the response.*

- *Help your teen to reach his goals by taking an active interest in them yourself. Ask questions that support your child's knowledge of himself and his dreams.*

- *Help your teen see herself as the person she is becoming; she will strive to live up to those expectations. Focus on your child's gifts, not all the things they can't do well.*

Keeping the Faith

August, two years later . . .

I'm so excited to be starting college! The day I thought would never come is actually here. Patience is a virtue, I guess. Graduation was a blast, after all. It almost made these last four years worth it. Now that it's all done I realize that there was a lot of good mixed in with the bad. I'm going to miss my friends so much. I love them all! Who knows what kind of friends I'll make at college? Lots to look forward to. And I guess there's also a lot to look back on. I hate to admit it, but I'm going to miss the way Mom and Dad always tried to protect me, even though it made me so mad sometimes. As excited as I am, I'm a little scared too. I feel like I've just finished the biggest challenge of my life, and now something even bigger is about to start. College. I hope the boys are a little more mature. Probably not. I wonder if the dorms get MTV? I wonder what my English professor will be like? I know I'm going to major in literature, even if Dad's making me keep my options open freshman year. What's the point? When you know, you know. I'm still scared. I hope I make some friends.

*   *   *

T he car cruised steadily down Interstate 80, carrying Greg, Kathy, and Kelly toward one of life's major intersections: The day your child arrives at college. The three had passed the time remembering Kelly's other major landmarks, including her first day of kindergarten. They had a laugh remembering Kelly's astonishment when her teacher forced her to spit out a piece of gum—while the flavor was still in it!

As their laughter settled down, Greg made a left onto a long drive and said, "Looks like we made it."

"I'm so excited!" Kelly said.

"We're excited for you!" Kathy told her.

An hour and a half later the three had finished unpacking the car and setting up Kelly's room, and stood lingering in front of the dorm.

"Well, I guess that about does it," Greg said, rubbing his hands together.

"Your roommate seems nice," Kathy said to Kelly.

"Yeah, she does."

There was a moment of silence during which no one knew quite what to say. Leaves whirled across the field in front of the dorm. And then Kelly threw an arm around each of her parents, buried her head in Greg's chest, and said, "I love you guys."

"We love you, too," they replied in unison.

After a moment Greg drew Kelly's chin up, and looking in her eyes discovered she was crying.

"Don't be sad," he told her.

"I'm not sad," she said. "I'm happy."

Greg and Kathy beamed. They were so proud to be seeing their little girl all grown up and going off to college.

"Remember," Greg said, "if you get sick, go straight to the infirmary. No boys in the room after dark. I put a calling card in your care package, so no excuses for not staying in touch. And, remember that we believe in you."

"Dad," Kelly said, "I'm not a two-year-old."

"What your father *means,* Kelly, is that we love you." Kathy smiled and twirled a lock of Kelly's hair in her finger. "You're going to do great, girl!"

After a few more hugs, Greg and Kathy finally managed to break themselves apart from their daughter without completely breaking down, and made their way back to the car.

"It's only a three-hour drive," Greg said, as he pulled back onto the highway. "I'm sure we'll still see her all the time."

"So," Kathy said, smiling, "now that it's happened, how does it feel to see our little girl all grown up?"

"Honestly," Greg told her, "kind of bittersweet."

"I know what you mean," Kathy said. "These last two years have been great. It's hard to believe Kelly's off on her own, making her own decisions. Let's just hope we did a good job."

"I think we've done a *great* job—both of us. After all, we've done the best we can. And if you think these last two years have been great, think of the two to come, and the two after that! Think of this as a new beginning."

"That's a good point," Kathy said. "There's a whole new set of rules now."

"The way I see it," Greg responded, "is that the exact opposite is true. Kelly *will* decide for herself, just like she always has. And our rules for ourselves haven't changed a bit. We'll still be there for her—no matter what. We always will be. I'm sure there'll be new challenges, but our job as committed parents hasn't changed."

"You're right. As far as we've come, we've got at least that far to go."

"Sure do," Greg said.

"Scared?" Kathy asked.

"Not a bit. Anxious, maybe. But I think we're ready for whatever comes along. The worst thing that happened my freshman year was that I was caught drinking in my dorm room. I think we've got that base covered."

Kathy laughed. "You're right. And think of all the problems we still have to face with Billy."

"Turns 15 next month," Greg said. "And something tells me that day he played hooky won't be the last."

"True." Kathy sighed. "Ready to ramp up the teenage coping skills again?"

"Ready as I'll ever be. But after all we've learned with Kelly, I think patience, commitment, and communication will help us carry Billy through whatever's ahead."

"I know it will," Kathy said.

* * *

A couple of months later, Greg came home late from work to find the house empty. He settled into his favorite chair and decided to catch up on some paperwork, rather than wait for the weekend. After only a few minutes he heard the garage door slam, followed by loud shouts.

Greg immediately started making his way to the kitchen. He could hear the shouting: "So what? It doesn't matter!" and "Don't give *me* that attitude." Greg walked swiftly into the kitchen and saw Kathy standing there fuming, her face red. "What's going on?" he asked.

"Our son was just cited for driving without a license."

"I have a permit," Billy said bluntly.

Greg's head began to reel. "Wait . . . what?" he said. "You took our car without permission . . . with only a learner's permit?" He was trying not to yell, but he couldn't even begin to imagine what had gotten into his son. Where was the trust? After a moment he turned to Kathy and asked, "What happened?"

Kathy shrugged, bewildered. "I got a call at work today around four o'clock, asking me to come down to the police station and pick up my son. Apparently they pulled him over for swerving on Thompson Lane."

Greg looked sternly at his son.

"We were just goofing around, Dad."

"Yeah, goofing around—in *my* car."

Billy went silent.

"So what are they going to do with him?" Greg asked.

"I don't know," Kathy replied. "Community service, I suppose. And I'm sure he won't be able to get his license for quite a while, either."

"Screw that!" Billy said.

"Enough!" Greg boomed. "Don't talk that way to your mother. And consider your driving privileges suspended indefinitely—no matter what the judge says. Believe me, that's nothing compared to the punishment you're going to get around here."

Billy pointed at his father and looked at him through squinted, angry eyes. "I don't care what you say. I'm fifteen years old! I'm gonna do whatever the hell I want!"

Greg was about to snap, but instead took a deep breath and stormed off into his den. What was that kid thinking? Did he think at all? Greg sighed loudly. "One thing's for sure," he thought, "Billy will never get anywhere with that attitude." Greg slumped into the chair at his desk and happened to notice he had new email. Opening his in box, Greg discovered a message from Kelly.

Dear Mom and Dad, she wrote.

How are things at home? Everything's fine here. I got a B+ on my last English test! The dorm food is still awful! but I'm doing all right. Better than my roommate, anyway. Her father came to visit this afternoon and apparently didn't realize that she's majoring in music. Claire has an incredible voice. She can sing everything! Britney Spears, Celine Dion, even opera. Growing up, she sang in her church choir and all of her high school's musicals. Anyway, her father came up today and found her desk with all her sheet music on it. I could almost see the steam coming out of his ears. I went out in the hallway, but I heard the yelling anyway. It was so sad. He just went on and on about how he'd sent her to college to study accounting, and how she was throwing her life away, and music was a waste of time. But she really is amazing. I mean, how will she know if she can make it if she doesn't even try? But her father doesn't understand that, apparently. After he left I went back in the room and Claire was crying. She said she tried everything—she even offered to sing him something—but he wouldn't listen. I guess he told her to switch majors at semester break or drop out for good. What a total jerk! I hope it doesn't come to that. I'd hate to see her leave, but I'd also hate to see her give up her dream. Anyway, this whole thing gave me a lot to think about. I mean, I'm planning on majoring in what I love and have all this great support from you guys. I'd hate to have to fight like that just to follow my passion. I just wanted you guys to know that I'm really, really glad you've been supportive. College is a lot of pressure as it is, and I realize I'm lucky that you guys support my choices. It means a lot to me. I miss you guys.

Love, Kelly

The email brought a smile to Greg's face, and a tear to his eye. Kelly was a good kid. She'd started out that way from the very beginning, just like Billy had. Greg and Kathy had helped her through some difficult years and gotten her off to college. And here she was, already blossoming into the amazing adult they'd seen in her all along. Greg almost laughed, thinking back five minutes to his pained thoughts that Billy might never make it in the world.

After all he'd been through, all he'd changed in himself, and all he'd learned, how could he fail to help his son? Greg leaned back and realized that the roadblocks ahead would be new, and more numerous than he would like. But he was ready to meet the challenges head on. He knew that with his and Kathy's love and commitment, Billy would eventually grow into a fine man. He remembered the words of his own father, many years ago:

"Good times, as well as bad times, don't last forever. Enjoy the journey. The teenage years also end."

What to Remember

- *Be patient in your parenting process. It may take years to see the results of your efforts.*

- *The future always holds new problems and challenges. The best way to address these is to anticipate them, and to be committed to working through them positively.*

- *"Keep the faith; don't give it away." —Mary Chapin Carpenter*

WOULD YOU LIKE TO

relate better to your teen

AND HAVE YOUR TEEN RELATE BETTER TO YOU?

Parent or Teen Coaching can be helpful to almost any parent or teenager who needs to stay focused and motivated. Coaching can also help you make good decisions in relating to one another. Like a personal fitness trainer, a coach can give both of you individualized attention to help you assess your social and personal strengths as well as identify and eliminate your weaknesses (i.e., blind spots).

The ultimate goal of coaching is to help bring out the absolute best in both of you so that you can bring out the best in each other. Whether you get coaching for yourself or your teen, remember, there is still hope.

For more information about our Parent or Teen Coaching services, contact us at

LifeBound
1600 Broadway, Suite 2400
Denver, CO 80202
info@lifebound.com
303-542-1811

Mention this book when you write or call and get a 30-minute session absolutely FREE!

GIVE US 45 MINUTES AND WE'LL HELP YOU

understand your teenager

BETTER THAN YOU EVER HAVE BEFORE

Dear Friend,

Here are a few of our favorite quotes we share with parents:

> *"Parenting is a lifelong process—it should only stop when you do."*
>
> —*Dr. Denis Kimbro*

> *"Experience may be a GOOD teacher, but other people's experience is a BETTER teacher."*
>
> —*Prof. Joe Martin*

> *"What you learn to do today will determine what your family becomes tomorrow."*
>
> —*Unknown*

After spending countless hours reflecting on how to help parents MOTIVATE, INSPIRE, and CONNECT with their teenagers, and at the same time prevent "PARENT BURN-OUT" in what we consider to be the TOUGHEST job in the world (raising a teenager), we decided to take action and make it virtually impossible for you to fail.

We've done all the work for you and made it easy for you to connect with your teenager on an emotional level, while at the same time reduce your stress level as a parent!

"The Parent Power Tape of the Month Club!"™

Our mission with this monthly tape series is simple . . .

To help parents succeed who are COMMITTED to helping their teenagers succeed!

Every month, we will provide you with an audiotape consisting of an interview with a "real teenager" who voluntarily wants to share what today's teenagers (like yours) are going through. You get to listen in as each teen reveals to YOU the things most parents don't know, but wish they knew, about their teenager.

These are REAL TEENAGERS (not actors). Now you can finally find out what teenagers are really thinking on a variety of issues that are most important to you! We've asked them the tough questions, and they've given us painfully honest answers. We know how valuable this information is and how much you value your time, so we made it affordable and easy to accommodate any parent's budget and busy schedule. Your minimum investment is only $9.95 (50% off the regular price $19.90) per month. Now you can gain instant access into the minds of YOUR teenagers without invading their privacy. Being part of this exclusive club of parents couldn't be easier! Your credit card is automatically billed each month (tax deductible for educational purposes), and the monthly tape is automatically delivered to your mailbox with NO WORK ON YOUR PART (all the work has been done for you)! You can cancel your subscription at anytime and keep the tapes you have.

You simply pop the tape in your cassette player, and in less than 60 minutes, you'll be informed, in touch, and inspired with the insight you'll gain—ready to strengthen your relationship with your teenager! You can even share the tapes with your teenager to open up the lines of communication.

See the following page for easy enrollment!

"Being part of this exclusive club is a no-brainer!"

"We've done all the work for you. We've made it easy and cost effective for you to gain access to real teenagers from all over the country!"

"Our relationships will NOT improve until WE improve!"

"Don't just sit there—enroll today!"

—The Parent Coaches

Reasons Why You Should Join!

Get inspired by learning from real teenagers!

Help other parents by getting them enrolled!

Save money and time (less than a parenting seminar)!

Stay motivated when the going gets tough!

Get timely information from teens on: peer pressure, teenage stress, drug/alcohol issues, parent pressure, teen relationships, grades, rebellious behavior, and much, much more . . . every month!

The authors of *Stop Parenting & Start Coaching* introduce their exclusive . . .

Parent Power Tape of the Month Club™

LEARN HOW TO SUCCEED AS A PARENT AS YOU HELP YOUR TEENAGER SUCCEED IN LIFE!

"Yes . . . Count me in. I see the incredible value in being a member of your exclusive club of parents, and I'm taking advantage of this chance to enroll in your Parent Power Tape of the Month Club. I want to receive a special teenage interview cassette each month for the low investment of $~~19.90~~ per month . . . "

Special offer of only $9.95 per month . . . 50% off and a savings of more than $114.00 per year! Bonus: It's also tax deductible.

print clearly

Name: _____

Tel #: _____ Email: _____

Address: _____

City: _____ State: _____ Zip: _____

Payment: ☐ Visa ☐ Master Card
☐ Check *(pay $100 one time for the year, and save an additional $20)*

Payable to: RealWorld University, 2732 McFarlane Court, Tallahassee, FL 32303

Card #: _____ Exp. Date: _____

Print name as it appears on card: _____

I authorize the above amount to be charged to the above credit card (I can cancel at anytime):

Signature: _____ Date: _____

(required for credit card authorizations)

FAX THIS FORM ANY TIME 24 HOURS A DAY to (707) 248-7421
Or call in your order to 1-850-212-0227 (M–F, 9:00 AM–5:00 PM EST)

Other Success Books by These Authors

The following books are available through
Prentice Hall Publishers.
Visit www.prenhall.com (search by keywords "keys to").

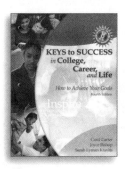  

The following books are available through LifeBound.
Visit www.lifebound.com

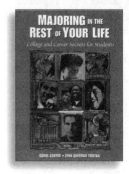

The following books are available through
RealWorld University Publishing.
Visit www.RWuniversity.com

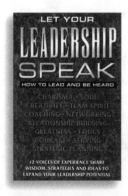